praise for
rethinking tourism and ecotravel

"Reading this book will make us all better tourists."
—Rebecca L. Adamson, President
FIRST NATIONS DEVELOPMENT INSTITUTE

"Anyone who has experienced the tawdry side of tourism—and most travelers have—will find this compelling reading. It is a superb insightful combination of personal anecdotes and documented research about the social and environmental problems generated by tourism. It enables the reader not only to grasp the magnitude of the negatives of tourism spawned economic growth, but also provides what must be done to correct them."
—D. Reber Dunkel, Ph.D
DEPARTMENT OF SOCIOLOGY AND ANTHROPOLOGY,
UNIVERSITY OF RICHMOND

"With a remarkable grasp of the downside of tourism, Ms. McLaren details how irresponsible tourism despoils the planet. She balances this sad story, however, by advocating responsible travel and suggests ways in which we may protect and respect all of creation."
—Virginia T. Hadsell
FOUNDER, CENTER FOR RESPONSIBLE TOURISM

"Guides the unsuspecting behind the glossy tourist brochures into the lives and fragile ecosystems of those who serve the largest industry. By opening the door wide on tourism, Deborah McLaren answers the questions no one asks; 'Who owns the industry? Who finances it? and How much of the proceeds stay in the local economy?' "
—John Cavanagh
CO-DIRECTOR, INSTITUTE FOR POLICY STUDIES
AND CO-AUTHOR OF GLOBAL DREAMS

rethinking tourism
and ecotravel

Kumarian Press

Selected Titles

Rethinking Tourism and Ecotravel:
The Paving of Paradise and What
You Can Do to Stop It
Deborah McLaren

Achieving Broad-Based Sustainable
Development: Governance,
Environment, and Growth with
Equity
*James H. Weaver, Michael T. Rock,
and Kenneth Kusterer*

Voices from the Amazon
Binka Le Breton

Bread, Bricks, and Belief:
Communities in Charge of
Their Future
Mary Lean

Down to Earth: Community
Perspectives on Health,
Development, and the Environment
*Bonnie Bradford and Margaret A.
Gwynne, editors*

When Corporations Rule the World
David C. Korten

Promises Not Kept: The Betrayal of
Social Change in the Third World,
Third Edition
John Isbister

Democratizing Development:
The Role of Voluntary
Organizations
John Clark

The Human Farm: A Tale of
Changing Lives and Changing
Lands
Katie Smith

Intermediary NGOs: The
Supporting Link in Grassroots
Development
Thomas F. Carroll

Getting to the 21st Century:
Voluntary Action and the
Global Agenda
David C. Korten

rethinking tourism
and ecotravel

___ — ___

the paving of paradise
and what you can do to stop it

Deborah McLaren

Kumarian Press

This book is dedicated
to a new generation of activists,

Shawnee, Jordan Olivia, Andrew, Sarah, Emily Rose, and Zachary

*Rethinking Tourism and Ecotravel: The Paving of Paradise
and What You Can Do to Stop It*

Published 1998 in the United States of America by Kumarian Press, Inc.,
14 Oakwood Avenue, West Hartford, Connecticut 06119-2127 USA.

Production supervised by Jenna Dixon
Copyedited by Linda Lotz   Proofread by Beth Richards
Typeset by CompuDesign
Index prepared by Douglas Easton

The text of this book is set in 10.5/13 Monotype Electra.
The display type is Fontek La Bamba.
Printed in Canada on acid-free paper by
Transcontinental Printing and Graphics, Inc.

Text printed with vegetable-based ink.
⊗ The paper used in this publication meets the minimum requirements of the
American National Standard for Information Sciences—Permanence of Paper for
Printed Library Materials, ANSI Z39.48-1984.

Library of Congress Cataloging-in-Publication Data
McLaren, Deborah, 1959–
    Rethinking tourism and ecotravel : the paving of paradise and what you can do to stop it
/ Deborah McLaren.
        p.   cm.
    Includes bibliographical references (p.   –   ) and index.
    ISBN 1-56549-066-5 (cloth : alk. paper) — ISBN 1-56549-065-7 (paper : alk. paper)
    1. Ecotourism. I. Title.
G155.A1M388   1998
338.4'791—dc21   97-15016

07 06 05 04 03 02 01 00   10 9 8 7 6 5 4 3 2
1st Printing 1998

contents

acknowledgments

This book would not be possible without the wisdom, prayers, and encouragement of many people, especially my editor, Trish Reynolds, production manager Jenna Dixon, and everyone at Kumarian Press. Special thanks also to Vincent Di Blasi, Dan Chodorkoff, Karen Conner, Annie Kriska, Bahe Rock, Ed Hall, Nilo Cuyuqueo, Steve Gorelick, Glenn Switkes, Jim Epstein, RTP board members, Andy Fisher, Stephen Kelleher, Virginia Hadsell, Kay Treakle, Dr. Eklabya Sharma, Juan Aulestia and Cathy Walsh, Gerry Colby and Charlotte Dennett, Daphne Wysham, Alicia Korten, Annie Leonard, André Carothers, Stephen Dix, Shelley Attix, Marjorie Deck, Reber Dunkel, Ron Mader, Luciano Minerbi, Bob Peregoy, Tomo Sasaki, Geetanjali Tiwari, Nazir Ahmad, Bambi Krauss, Melina Selverston, Maria Augusta Espinoza, Elaine Broadhead, John Ackerly, Deborah Tull, Paul Gonsalves, Peter Holden, and friends at National Writers Union, at the Institute for Policy Studies, Indigenous and Native groups, and in the responsible tourism movement.

Thanks to Clay Hubbs, editor of *Transitions Abroad* magazine, who encouraged critical analysis of the tourism industry through my column for many years and who provided editorial expertise for this book. Others who gave incredible amounts of their time, asked lots of tough questions, and provided editorial skills as well as inspiration include Nadine Granoff, Leigh Hammill, Annie Scarborough, Naomi Friedman, Leah Barry, and Leon Gendin. I'm also indebted to Shmuel Ben-Gad at the George Washington University Gelman Library and to Clay Butler for the use of his insightful cartoons.

I want to thank my family, who taught me the value of travel. I especially thank my mother, Patsy Ann Rillo, who never gave a second thought about spending summers camping along the Natchez Trace or going to powwows; and my father, Dale McLaren, a very global traveler. My stepparents also provide international cultural perspectives, from the Philippines and Singapore, that enrich my life and thinking. Thanks to Ken, Jamie, Robert, Nicky, Maria, Scott, and Laura, who have shared many travels and cross-cultural experiences with me.

My thanks also to the many individuals who welcomed me into their lives and taught me about how tourism affects them and what they are doing to change it: Renzino Lepcha, Marcia Valerezo, Leonardo Viteri, Cesar Cerde, Dave Lacey, Randy Mayo, Chayant Pholphoke, Ivy Wong Puisee, Helena Norberg-Hodge and the Ladakhi people, Lisert Prasert, Dev Singh Gurung, Luis and Luz Macas, Harka Gurung, Jarot Sumarwoto, Dianne Brause, and others.

Thank you, Creator.

prologue:

a personal journey

my reasons for supporting change in the tourism industry came about through personal experience. I began to think about taking a vacation to Jamaica many years ago. I had heard about the island all my life and looked forward to going there. As a child, I had watched home movies of my missionary grandfather working in Jamaica. I particularly remember a film where twenty or so people were dancing outside under some trees; what most struck me was the spirit and joyousness the people projected.

My interest in Jamaica and Jamaican culture continued to take various turns over the years. During the early 1970s, when I was growing up in a small town in northeastern Oklahoma, some of my friends started a band and began singing the reggae songs of Bob Marley. Living in an economically depressed rural area and grappling with social and cultural issues of my own, I could identify with the meaning and message of struggle. More than a decade later, with some experience behind me and enough money to make the trip, I went to Jamaica to look, idealistically, for a chance to better understand the meaning of the revolutionary spirit. What I found was very different from what I had imagined. I had not realized the depth of struggle against racism and oppression, the sheer poverty that many Jamaicans live with every day, the historical oppression and hardships the culture had experienced. I had simply glossed over much of it. I bought into the dream that I could go to Jamaica as a package-deal tourist and have a profound experience with local people.

In fact I did have a profound experience, but it was not the type for which I was searching. The plane landed at Montego Bay and I was

1

immediately besieged by hawkers and hustlers, self-styled entrepreneurs in an economic situation born directly out of the business of tourism. I didn't even have time to look around as I downed my welcome-to-Jamaica shot of rum because I was so preoccupied with the hustlers: "Like a beer for the ride, mon?" "Need some ganga, girl?" "You need a mon like John to show you around."

I stayed in a hotel arranged as part of a package deal with an airline. The resort was advertised as set in a "historical plantation in Old Jamaica"; its fences and golf course recalled a colonialist plantation, strong symbols of a time that never seemed to pass for some. It was a beautiful beach resort surrounded by imported comforts from home, while local people were banned from the beach and lived in a makeshift service village across the road. A sign near the fence at the end of the hotel beach said it all: "No Locals Allowed." The t-shirts and bikinis in the souvenir shop were imported from the United States; the restaurant's food was shipped in from Florida.

I didn't have much opportunity to meet local people on the "old plantation." Most were too busy working in their service jobs. One morning, determined to see a more genuine side of the island, I crossed the main road to take the local bus into Montego Bay. The guards at the gates of the hotel eyed me suspiciously. Some older women waiting for the bus cast an amused glance in my direction. A dilapidated school bus pulled up, and I boarded, along with the older women and a young man holding a live chicken. A hand-painted sign over the driver's seat reflected a contemporary social issue for Jamaicans, "Let us stay sober on our journey." My whole experience that day was one of hustlers, drug dealers, and more hustlers. I was unable to walk around without an offer for a "guide," to buy some "smoke," or to inspect a wood-carving shop. It was off-season, the tourism-dependent economy was in its downswing, and people were desperate. Shopkeepers even sent scouts out into the streets to round up tourists to bring back to their shops.

One evening I went to Montego Bay to hear some reggae music. After a considerable search, I finally found a small club for locals. As we listened to the music, a bus load of tourists rushed in and immediately began to complain to the deejay about the music. Soon Michael Jackson, Madonna, and Whitney Houston began to croon over the speakers while the tourists danced. After an hour or so, the tourists left and the American pop tunes were put to rest until the next round of tourists descended on the club. "The tourists," explained the deejay, "they like American music." The revolutionary songs of Bob Marley had no place in a carefree holiday market that depends upon providing pleasure for wealthy foreigners.

Throughout the rest of my stay in Jamaica, I tried to meet some local people without being accosted by entrepreneurs. But I was taken to other all-inclusive resorts around the island and to "destinations" like Dunns River Falls, where I climbed the waterfalls with other tourists and didn't see one local Jamaican on vacation. Instead, I saw the social discrepancies that distanced tourists from the local population. I noticed the way the residents reacted to me as a wealthy tourist with money to burn. I noticed the creation of a fantasy tourism culture that by no means represented the real culture of Jamaica. I noticed the almost entirely British and American management at the hotels. I noticed the dying reefs just off the beaches, polluted from unregulated waste from the resorts; the high price of black coral, disappearing quickly because of the excessive demand by tourists; the stench from piles of accumulated garbage behind the beautiful, artificial resorts; pristine lands being converted into more tourist accommodations; and fences that blocked the local people from the beach.

On my last day in Jamaica, I walked down the road to a horse stable where I met Joseph, a guide. While we rode around the hillside through villages conspicuously different from the hotel paradises I had been a part of, Joseph related some of his story. He had grown up in Jamaica and spent four years as a worker on cruise and fishing boats traveling throughout the Caribbean and to ports in Europe. Joseph was interested in people. In fact he said it was this interest that motivated him to work on the boats and was why he was currently employed as a guide at the stables. He wanted to see the world, especially the United States, where, Joseph said, "people have more opportunities, . . . do not have to live in poverty. In the United States, people have good jobs and a good way of life that is better than here in Jamaica." He told me he was devastated when he was laid off from his job on a cruise ship just before it was scheduled to go to the United States. He had looked forward to the trip for years, and his disappointment was still visible. His interest in the United States had nonetheless continued to grow since then. As we rode our horses through a shantytown, Joseph made a remark about his missed opportunity that struck me. "Oh well," he said, "I will prepare myself so that I will understand more when I go there."

My time with Joseph is one of my best memories of the trip: it was a human connection, even if the unequal guide-tourist relationship prevented a real friendship from developing and even if we both had stereotyped views of each other. The very nature of tourism created in each of us idealized images of each other's culture: my perception of Jamaica was one of happy revolutionaries; his perception of the United States was one of wealthy vacationers with no responsibilities at home. The tourism industry enforced and encouraged the distance between tourists and locals and reinforced a negative self-image for Joseph. It offered no mechanisms for fostering friendships with locals or gaining insight into local cultures, and I was hampered in my own attempts. I wanted to tell Joseph that the United States wasn't the utopia he thought it was, but who was I to talk? Since then I have thought about Joseph's wise words many times. I decided to prepare myself for the realities of whatever culture I might visit and to find ways to represent myself more realistically.

Over the years I have continued to learn from my experience in Jamaica. I was not able to contact much real Jamaican culture because of the culture that tourism had imposed. Why did it seem as though tourism controlled Jamaica and Jamaica had no control over tourism? I am disturbed by my own projections of a culture and people that exist only as a commodity, cooked up and dished out by the travel industry and the media. How did this happen? Did the colonial plantation-cum-resort where I stayed represent a larger, more controversial phenomenon, something still being perpetrated?

My participation as a tourist propelled me into a process of critical analysis and a conscious effort to support change within the tourism industry. From this perspective, my goal is to demonstrate how traditional tourism, especially in countries in the global South (so-called developing countries in the Southern Hemisphere), basically follows a consumption-oriented Western model. The overwhelming growth of tourism has been destructive to both ecology and people in host countries.

There is a desperate need for information and tools to create change. I've learned to look past immediate tourism issues for root causes—to world economics, the media and technologies, development models, corporate control, the continuation of colonization, racism, and other forms of injustice. My exploration of tourism issues has been difficult, alarming, and wonderful and has led me to look for ways to change, challenge, and sometimes completely denounce the industry.

This book focuses on the global tourism industry and the recent boom in ecotravel. Tourism is inherently about our earth. Vacations at lakeside camps, at ski resorts, and in national parks reflect the need for human beings to spend time in nature. It's obvious that the global tourism industry has an enormous impact on the environment and in most cases sells nature as part of the tourist product. We cannot simply buy into the eco-jargon. What we need is an overview of tourism that acknowledges that "green" travel, or ecotravel, is a mere part of the larger impact of the industry and that there is an urgent need to look at the broad issues related to tourism's impacts upon the earth.

There is increasing resistance to tourism. Some of it has simply been to "greenwash" tourism and promote it as a sustainable development strategy or as "cultural heritage" that enshrines past culture and negates current culture. Since the 1970s, however, local people have joined with ecumenical groups, Indigenous Peoples, women's groups, grassroots groups, environmentalists, and even tourists to challenge and denounce the negative impacts of global tourism and seek alternatives in an international "responsible tourism" movement. Growing numbers of organizations outside of but reliant upon the travel industry are also rethinking their roles in tourism and creating strategies for change. Some of these groups are organizing solidarity tours to pressure governments and support each other at the grassroots level; others are linking with each other on social justice issues.

Thousands of communities around the world are attempting some form of tourism development. Many people in communities where abrupt transformations are taking place have little information about the forces changing their lives. What is apparent, though, is that most of the communities are going through almost entirely the same process: fairly well defined cycles of expectation and disappointment. Yet tourism continues to grow haphazardly, often to the detriment of local people, communities, and the environment, with little long-term, integrated planning.

The Westernized model of unlimited economic growth has driven multinational aid and financial institutions since the 1940s, yet poverty has increased, arable lands are shrinking and threatened, and the socioeconomic situation of most of the world is worse than ever. World leaders are now organizing international meetings to determine what to do about preserving our global commons, the air we breathe and the water we drink, natural elements that cross borders—and that we all depend upon to survive. While there is growing interest in other cultures, there are also backlashes against ethnic groups. Our capacity to learn and to work for change has never been more promising, yet the issues and solutions are dauntingly complex. In trying to protect our precious natural resources, we must look at both energy-consumptive high technologies and localized, less consumptive strategies.

The effects of travel and tourism development are usually studied in bits and pieces. For instance, environmentalists typically scrutinize the negative effects of tourism development upon natural resources and have focused primarily on conservation issues. Economists concentrate upon business, employment, trade, and financial issues. Anthropologists document changing tribal cultures, some on the verge of vanishing. In the United States, we tend to study the global South as a separate entity, although we have recently come to learn that its survival is directly tied to the survival of the industrialized nations of the North. We must begin to explore the overlapping issues of tourism development and its effects upon the earth and society through a more integrated approach. Tourists are becoming increasingly concerned about the impact of their travel and the control of the giant tourism industry, and they are looking for information and tools to assist them in becoming more responsible travelers and bringing about change within the industry.

But is there any reason to work to change tourism, or should we stop traveling altogether? Concepts for alternative tourism as well for *alternatives to* tourism reflect the growing awareness of the importance of cultural preservation and ecological protection and decentralized political and economic decisionmaking. These factors are critical, especially as the era of exploitive free trade and globalization of the economy intensifies. In the struggle to return control of tourism to the local community, we must increasingly scrutinize our motives for traveling, decide whether we have the "right" as consumers to buy other cultures and environments, and support responsible tourism. We must analyze "green" strategies such as ecotourism and sustainable tourism to determine whether we are simply being "greenwashed." In an age where the media dominate and shape our views of the world, it is imperative that we utilize tourism as a means to communicate with one another. In fact there is no better way to understand the global crisis that we face than through people-to-people communication. Through firsthand, one-on-one meetings with people we encounter in our travels, we discover universal themes of human culture. We become more aware that no matter where we live, we are all confronting similar situations. Even nature travel is in many ways a reconnection between postindustrialized society and Mother Earth.

The issue of growth in the travel industry—how much, how fast, what kind—is crucial to the future of communities, local lifestyles and cultures, and the natural environment. There are a variety of instabilities and inequities associated with the expansion of tourism. If the social costs of infinite growth (human consequences of ecological pollution, centralized concentration of power, inequitable income distribution) are as high as they appear to be, our current social systems cannot support such growth indefinitely. Tourism remains a passive luxury for thousands of travelers. This must change.

This book excludes large sectors of the travel industry, such as business travel and conferences and travel to most urban and developed areas. It focuses instead on tourism that affects areas where planned "development" has had a short history. There are many tourism subjects that I do not adequately address in this book, such as how specific corporations are involved in tourism, how tourism can be linked to organized crime, and state policies on tourism.

I present here a starting point for rethinking a phenomenal industry, the largest in the world. This book is an invitation to undertake tourism-related studies and actions on issues such as agriculture, technologies, exploitation of women and children, and the role of transnational corporations. I look forward to future works that will engage these issues from other points of view and with different emphases. The purpose of my book is to encourage further investigation and action on the part of the reader.

Where will tourists be traveling in the next century? Will there be any places left to "discover?" Or will our search for unspoiled environments and cultures be in vain, as they become replaced by manufactured cultures on reconstructed islands of paradise? If the megamall, theme park, and cruise ship are any indication of our future, "supertourists" who can afford it may pay to visit the last pristine places on the planet, to view the history of the Indigenous Peoples and organic agriculture, admire what used to be rain forests, and watch "virtual" cultural entertainment. Perhaps they will visit private, enclosed biospheres or even the moon. Of course there will be plenty of souvenirs for them to buy.

1

an overview of tourism

human beings have migrated across the planet for millennia. Plate tectonics, feet, and horses made for slow travel compared to the jet planes, trains, and automobiles we now use. No doubt our ancestors would be surprised at the infinite options we modern travelers enjoy. The earliest hunters and gatherers and nomads traveled in search of land and wildlife to sustain themselves; they were aware of the fragility of the earth and moved with the seasons. Travel that stemmed from basic survival was, of course, very different from the travel we undertake today. Only during the past few decades have higher incomes and paid holidays in the global North allowed great numbers of people to travel purely for pleasure and recreation.

Tourism began in part as an offshoot of religious pilgrimages and colonization. Vikings traveled across vast seas for natural resources. Traders traveled throughout Europe, North Africa, and the Middle East in search of spices and other goods. During the seventeenth century, young elites took "grand tours" through Europe to expand their educational and cultural horizons; the most privileged took two to three years to see the world. Civil and secular authorities traveled to participate in events the church deemed historical or went on special missions accompanied by large entourages that often included cooks, attendants, guides, and porters. Religious pilgrimages made on horseback and in coaches during the Enlightenment stimulated the growth of inns. Around the turn of the nineteenth century, Europeans journeyed to view scenery and other cultures.

Authors such as Somerset Maugham and Joseph Conrad wrote romantic accounts of the Far East and the heart of Africa. Travel heroes like

Hemingway recounted their journeys to the lands of "savages," to hunt game, and their sea voyages in search of paradise. These conquering and self-indulgent adventurers brought along servants to make the trips comfortable. Few people could afford these exotic ventures into the wild, but some of these conquering ideals live on and constitute eco- and ethnocentrism that underlies much of modern tourism.

Naturalists such as Alexander von Humboldt and later Charles Darwin studied wildlife and plant species in exotic places and contributed greatly to an interest in travel. In the United States around the turn of the century, John Muir began to write about his wanderings overland through the southern states and journeys to Alaska and India. His trips made him an impassioned conservationist, and his work continues to inspire and mobilize people to preserve the natural world. Also about that time, a chain of national parks and other protected areas was created, partly in response to the fear that industrialization would consume them and partly to set aside unique lands to be shared by all citizens. Also in this century anthropologists like Margaret Mead drew global attention to Indigenous societies. Nature and cultural travel have continued to play an important role in conflicts between conservationists and economists and the public and private sectors.

The views of land and place held by travelers and hosts, colonizers and original inhabitants, have varied widely, and the compulsion of newcomers to take control of their "discoveries" and the resources and people they find there is striking. The conquest of paradise, colonization, and "discovery" were historic rationalizations to take over new lands. Today most land, even what is perceived as "open" land, is not understood to be part of an intricate system of land use and maintenance, the residents using the resources for survival rather than importing goods. These areas, often multiple use lands, and our global commons are threatened by increasing development and exploitation of natural resources.

the emergence of modern tourism

The transition from a rural to an industrial society encouraged the growth of modern tourism. Before World War II, travel for pleasure was the province of the very rich. Since then, improved standards of living in the Northern Hemisphere and the availability of transportation have allowed more people to indulge. Modern tourism began in large part with the rise of the automobile industry and expanded road and highway systems.

Early jet travel was generally confined to the United States and Europe, but by the 1960s improvements in aircraft technology opened up the world to visitors. The development of commercial jet airlines enabled fast international travel, and the tourism industry exploded. From 1945 to 1996, international arrivals alone increased from 25 million to 528 million, with industry analysts predicting more than 1 billion arrivals by the year 2000[1]. Today airports in nearly every country in the world can accommodate jumbo jets full of tourists seeking new and unspoiled destinations.

Travel to "exotic" places is increasingly popular. Travelers are searching out the most remote places as well as the most unusual cultures. Ethnic tourism, involving visits to villages and homes to observe social customs and traditional occupations such as fishing and farming, see (and purchase) native arts, and watch local ceremonies is one of the fastest-growing segments of the consumer travel market. New forms of environmental tourism are often related to ethnic tourism, marketing exotic cultures and areas where few have traveled.

These specialized segments of tourism are often excluded from analyses of the tourism industry. In economic terms, exotic cultures and unspoiled environments have become tourism's commodities. Although Indigenous populations and pristine environments are tourist attractions and important players in the industry, until recently they were rarely considered in tourism research, planning, development, and economics. There is some debate over using monetary economics for measuring gains and losses in the business of tourism. Tourism researchers are beginning to call culture and environment the supply side of tourism.

Tourism doesn't just package and sell products and services, such as transportation, accommodations, food, and a good time. It also sells beaches, mountains, and other natural sites, as well as cultures and people. The problem is that tourist businesses often do not own what they sell. Businesses in the industry purchase at inappropriately low prices, acquire free of charge, or simply expropriate these resources as part of their products. For example, when a developer builds a resort near a national park, part of the developer's product becomes the use of the park and all its natural attractions.

Tourism is often in direct conflict and competition with local people and communities, for it markets and develops natural resources the locals need. Because tourism requires an enormous amount of land, water, and energy, residents must fight the tourism industry and governments for land and water rights. Development of areas around the periphery also threatens wildlife in the entire bioregion.

DEBORAH MCLAREN, SIKKIM, INDIA

Traditional architecture in the Himalayas uses materials natural to the area that are flexible and able to withstand frequent earthquakes.

With rapidly expanding tourism development, multi-storied concrete structures are dangerously built and degrade fragile mountain environments.

DEBORAH MCLAREN, SIKKIM, INDIA

As tourism boosts demand for land, the cost of livable space increases, local people are displaced, and less space is available for sustainable lifestyles. Developers are notorious for filling in swamps, mangroves, and coral reefs, causing a chain reaction that hurts fishing, reduces the supply of fresh water for irrigation, and shrinks the land base. Local people are increasingly confined to infertile lands and degraded environments in nearby service cities. Ultimately, developers re-create the environment and culture on top of the real thing. These manufactured environments and cultures peddle the fiction that the corporations care for us and that we have earned the "right" to this short-term, expensive fantasy.

tourism as big business

In a shrinking world of improved travel facilities and computer linkages, a network of group travel and mass tourism continues to grow. The World Tourism Organization (WTO) claims that tourism is currently the world's largest industry. With annual revenues of almost $3 trillion, its economic impact is second only to that of the weapons industry. Between 1980 and 1989, expenditures on international travel alone, *excluding transportation*, doubled to $209 billion, rising one-third faster than the world gross national product. In the same time period, international tourism receipts more than doubled, from $10 billion to $230 billion, and by 1994 had increased to $321 billion. The WTO and other travel experts predict that world tourism will accelerate in many countries that have had little tourism experience to date, especially in the Pacific Rim; international tourist arrivals in developing countries have already increased 5 percent annually since the mid-1980s. Within the next few decades, tourism is expected to include space travel.

According to the WTO and Wharton Economic Forecasting Associates (the WEFA Group),

- by 1989 tourism was the third largest household expenditure after food and housing in most industrial nations;
- the industry employed more people than any other industrial sector (more than 112 million people, or one out of every fifteen workers worldwide);
- including lodging, transportation, and restaurants, the tourism infrastructure was worth $3 trillion;
- the industry had invested nearly $360 billion in new capital equipment.[2]

According to a White House report, "Travel is now America's largest business services export, generating a $22 billion trade surplus in 1993. It is also the second largest employer in the nation, providing jobs for over six million Americans."[3]

Tourism is larger than almost any single item in world trade and is growing at least 8 to 10 percent per year.[4] The travel industry has become a vast and complex enterprise that includes transportation (airlines, airports, trains, cruise lines, automobiles, and rental car agencies); hotels, resorts, and vacation villages; the food industry; travel agencies and operators; and recreational and cultural promoters such as trekking and adventure agencies. It also includes related tourism services such as trailer parks, campgrounds, and amusement and recreation parks, with their wholesale and retail shops (eating and drinking establishments and some apparel and accessory stores). Tourism is big business. And it is largely controlled by big business. Transnational corporations (TNCs) are involved not only in transportation and accommodations but in motivating us to travel, feeding and entertaining us while we are on vacation, making travel arrangements for us, providing us with "travel" money and insurance, plying us with souvenirs, and even outfitting us for our trips. According to a 1996 study, top tourism "holding" companies were Pepsi Company, which owns Pizza Hut, Taco Bell, and Kentucky Fried Chicken at $5.55 billion in annual sales; Marriott at $4.9 billion; McDonald's Corporation at $4 billion; and Disney (hotels and theme parks) at $605 million. Major airlines and their annual profits include Continental at $2.6 billion, Trans World Airlines (TWA) at $624 million, and Singapore Air at $510 million.[5]

International financial institutions are integrated into the global tourism industry. American Express, for example, combines financial and travel services for business and leisure services and controls a major share of the world market for traveler's checks. With deregulation of global financial systems, travelers have benefited from improvements in the speed and convenience of financial activities. We use our credit and automatic teller machine (ATM) cards around the world, particularly in the tourist sector. In a matter of seconds, we can obtain cash almost anywhere. These transactions are remarkable not only because they take place in remote sites but also because of the images they promote. A current television advertisement shows a young boy in an unspecified developing country leading a lost American couple through a desert village to an ATM. Another ad for MasterCard announces that it is now "uniting the world." These images are intended to illustrate how innovative, convenient, and caring the travel industry is.

Tourism is a mighty force in free trade agreements such as the General Agreement on Trade in Services (GATS), which promotes privatization and free trade and undermines the power of governments to protect and control their labor markets and resources. Economists tell us that "GATS will contribute to the worldwide development of tourism. It will also constrain—and should over time eliminate—government discrimination toward foreign service companies."[6] The key to liberalization, they say, is market access—granting foreign service suppliers access to domestic markets, including services—and "national treatment"—where countries are obliged to treat foreign tourist services suppliers in the same way they do domestic suppliers.

In reality, transnationals are breaking economic barriers that would regulate them, giving them more control of world markets and allowing them to ignore restrictions to protect workers and the environment. TNCs have no allegiance to any particular country; if they are in trouble in the United States because they have violated labor laws, for example, they can simply move to Mexico.

The multilateral development banks are investing heavily in tourism development around the global South as part of the foreign aid business. According to a recent report from the International Finance Corporation (IFC) and the World Bank, by 1994 the IFC had "approved close to $600 million in over 100 tourism projects. The tourism portfolio has grown at an average annual rate of over 23% over the past five years. [As of June 1994], the committed portfolio was $434 million in 66 projects."[7] Other international "players" in global tourism include intergovernmental organizations such as the World Health Organization; the International Civil Aviation Organization; the Organization of American States (OAS); the Organization for Economic Cooperation and Development (OECD); the Asia Pacific Economic Cooperation (APEC); the World Travel and Trade Council (WTTC); the Pacific Asia Travel Association (PATA); the World Trade Organization (WTO); and United Nations programs such as the United Nations Educational, Scientific, and Cultural Organization (UNESCO) and the United Nations Development Program (UNDP). The World Travel and Tourism Council, located in London, is a council of chief executive officers of private-sector companies involved in tourism. Their primary mandate is to affect government policy and business.

But the tourism industry also comprises businesses that originate outside of the organized economy, forming what is called the "open air" economy of tourism. These meager, insecure, and illegal operations often spring up as poor people migrate to tourist sites look for work. Because many of these jobs, such as the selling of drinks and fruit or running errands, are performed by children, the industry cannot account for them in its data. Many of these small operations are run by women and children pushed out by the giants in the industry.[8]

tourism and globalization

A traveler can decide today to go to the North Pole and be there by tomorrow. Global infrastructures such as transportation and communications and global policies for free trade have created a situation where people and businesses in the global North can easily access natural resources and cultures in the global South. Globalization is not regarded as a danger to local economies and cultural diversity. In fact it has been touted by politicians and the media as the path to greater wealth and success. Although globalization may be the most primary transformation of the world's political and economic structures since the industrial revolution, its implications have yet to be fully understood or debated.

Most of the economic restructuring is in the interest of big business, not in the interest of the public. Under the banner of free trade, corporations have come to shape our lives through the consumer products we buy (including technologies), the media that feed us information, even the educational system that trains us. Politicians chant the mantra of privatization and globalization. What does that mean for individuals? According to Martin Khor, president of the nongovernmental organization (NGO), Third World Network, globalization is a leading threat to local communities, particularly in the global South:

> Before colonial rule and the infusion of Western systems, people in the Third World lived in relatively self-sufficient communities. . . . The modes of production and style of life were largely in harmony with the natural environment. Colonial rule . . . changed the social and economic structures of Third World societies. The new structures, consumption styles, and technological systems became so ingrained in Third World economies that even after the attainment of political independence, the importation of Western values, products, technologies and capital continued and expanded. . . . Third World governments were loaned billions of dollars to finance expensive infrastructure projects. . . . They were also supported by foundations, research institutions, and scientists in the industrialized countries that carried out research on new agricultural technologies that would "modernize" the Third World—that is, that would create conditions whereby the Third World would become dependent on the transnational companies for technology and inputs.[9]

The development of vast infrastructures such as roads and other transportation routes goes hand in hand with tourism development. As more

PAVE THE PLANET

ONE ASPHALT, ONE PEOPLE

Sidewalk Bubblegum ©1993 Clay Butler

tourists seek out hard-to-reach "frontier" destinations, those areas become popularized, and soon private industry takes over. Once an area is targeted for tourism development, the process begins with road building and displacement of the local population. Communications systems go in, as do energy-intensive and pollutive accommodations for visitors. The roads and communications in turn provide other industries with easy access to cheap labor and natural resources. This cycle of development is occurring at alarming rates in small communities and villages throughout the world; many of these areas are considered the most important biologically diverse regions of the planet. At the same time, roads built into places like the Amazon to serve primarily as transportation routes for extractive industries such as oil, logging, and mining inevitably become new corridors for colonists, including tourists.

Tourism increases local reliance upon a global economy, leaking many economic profits outside of the community back to the companies and countries that control most of the travel infrastructure. At the same time, tourism decreases dependence on local resources, as technologies, food, and health services are imported. Local people may also be pushed out or sell out, and local prices for commodities and services rise, as do taxes.

Any number of groups and individuals are concerned about the negative impacts of economic centralization via free trade and regional agreements such as the General Agreement on Tariffs and Trade (GATT) and the European Union. These organizations point out that the promotion of greater economic units and the expanded transport infrastructures they require result in urbanization in the global North and South alike, placing greater pressures on wilderness areas and destroying family farms and rural communities around the world. Proponents of free trade promise that all trading partners will be better off and that the practice will usher in a new era of global cooperation and prosperity. But according to a report by the International Society for Ecology and Culture:

> The reality is far different. Increased levels of world trade will lead to a widening of the gap between rich and poor, to further environmental decline, and to the enrichment of corporations at the expense of people in both the North and South. Small farmers and shopkeepers will be driven under by producers and marketers whose activities are undertaken at an ever larger scale, and many local economies will simply not survive. Rural communities will be hardest hit, intensifying the trend toward urbanization. These "free trade" agreements are fundamentally anti-democratic. The ease with which corporations will be able to transcend national boundaries—to move wherever environmental and health standards are the weakest and wages lowest—will strip voters and even governments of their power to curb corporate excess. . . . In the new global economy, production everywhere will be focused on the needs of a single, Western, monoculture, while Indigenous cultures and diverse location-specific adaptations will be steadily erased. Local self-sufficiency will become an ever more distant memory.[10]

Tourism plays an increasingly important role in international relations. There are links between tourist flow and regional integration, governments, military, and economic aid. "Most nations have several policies toward foreign tourists that are based not only on anticipated length of stay, but also on the degree of international cooperation existing between the two countries."[11]

Tourism is big business for governments and private enterprise alike. Any country with still pristine areas of forests, beaches, mountains, and park lands or with ethnic tribes and other unique rural cultures has something to market in the global economy. Some of the largest corporations in the world are designing and carrying out policies that open up borders and allow them to operate in areas once restricted to individual country corporations. The tourist industry's entrance into and operations in China, the Middle East, the former Soviet Union, and countries with human rights abuses show that government and big business can work together despite trade restrictions and political differences. Corporations have become dominant governing institutions, often exceeding governments in size and power. As David Korten states, "Increasingly, it is the corporate interest more than the human interest that defines the policy agendas of states and international bodies, although this reality and its implications have gone largely unnoticed and unaddressed."[12] Nowhere is this more true than within travel and tourism.

Governmental instruments and international organizations that help shape international tourism policy encourage the growth and involvement of transnational corporations because they provide quick money and expanded trade and services. In supporting and increasing the power of such corporations, governments are ignoring the numerous inequalities, exploitation, and dislocations they foster. Countries create lax trade environments to attract the tourism industry, lifting restrictions that are applied to other industries and offering many incentives. Alexander Goldsmith explains that

> free trade zones [FTZs] are regions that have been fiscally or juridically redefined by their "host country" to give them a comparative advantage over neighboring regions and countries in luring transnational corporate activity. Most FTZs share the following characteristics: lax social, environmental, and employment regulations; a ready source of cheap labor; and fiscal and financial incentives that can take a huge variety of forms, although they generally consist of the lifting of customs duties, the removal of foreign exchange controls, tax holidays, and free land or reduced rents.[13]

The travel industry benefits greatly from these FTZs, sometimes even performing what may be considered "advance work" in doing away with free trade barriers for other industries.

international and national tourism regulations and policies

Both international agreements and national policies regulate tourism in the United States. Perhaps the best-known international pacts concerning tourism are the 1975 Helsinki Accord, which deals with the rights of people to migrate freely and of governments to increase tourism, and the Accord of Mutual Understanding and Cooperation in Sports, which discourages boycotts of the Olympic Games for political reasons.[14] The 1980 Manila Declaration and the Acapulco Charter are the primary international agreements on tourism to date, yet neither provides much beyond vague guidelines that "tourism resources should be managed and conserved" and "international cooperation, both financial and technological, should be encouraged." Almost all tourism agreements focus on the expansion and promotion of trade. Tourism is rarely recognized within the context of environmental and labor issues, although responsible tourism organizations and women's groups have pushed a plan demanding that countries observe the United Nations Convention on the Rights of the Child on behalf of children who are prostituted, enslaved, and trafficked internationally through tourism. However, the U.N. is beginning to design policies that include tourism and biodiversity protection, and the WTO recently released a declaration about social and environmental responsibilities of the tourism industry. Worldwide pressure from NGOs, Indigenous Peoples, and communities are responsible for pushing tourism issues to the forefront.

The United States began to develop a tourism policy in 1974 when a group of senators authorized the Senate Commerce Committee to undertake the National Tourism Policy Study, which was completed in 1978 and eventually became the National Tourism Policy Act of 1981. This act redefined the national interest in tourism and created the U.S. Travel and Tourism Administration (USTTA), until early 1997 the nation's government tourism office. The principal mission of the USTTA was to implement broad policy initiatives and develop tourism as a stimulus to the growth of the U.S. travel industry. The act also increased the importance of tourism policy within the U.S. Department of Commerce and established the Tourism Policy Council to promote tourism in federal decisionmaking. A second policy established the Travel and Tourism Advisory Board, which advised the secretary of commerce and focused on marketing.

The Tourism Policy and Export Promotion Act of 1992 set the stage for the direction of U.S. tourism policy; it targeted untapped markets and lesser-known destinations. The State Department has the primary role in establishing bilateral tourism agreements with nations. A 1993 Commerce Department report describes tourism as "embedded in . . . agreements designed and negotiated for broad trade and investment reasons. . . . Under these agreements, U.S. companies are generally guaranteed national treatment for establishing themselves in the other country for advertising and selling in the other market."[15] Numerous congressional hearings have focused on activities such as marketing tourism and using tourism to boost rural economic development. Although tourism is an intrinsic part of international trade policy, there are now fewer formal government tourism offices, as global corporations take over their function. According to the State Department, "In 1995, the U.S. government decided to withdraw from organizations such as the World Tourism Organization and private tourism companies such as Disney and Visa have become affiliate members instead."[16] In early 1997 the USTTA was virtually abolished. U.S. tourism policymakers and industry developers now belong to the Office of Tourism Industries, within the International Trade Administration's Trade Development Office. U.S. tourism has thus become part of the process of global trade liberalization. State offices are following the same course by dismantling their tourism offices.

tourism and development

The 1995 White House Conference on Tourism was a missed opportunity. The administration of Bill Clinton focused solely on the technological and economic potential of tourism and its role in promoting free trade. It made a commitment to protecting national parks, improving the campground reservation system and customer service, and funding scenic byways along U.S. highways. Yet it failed to see the broad environmental impact of the industry. The conference focused on economic growth, not on sustainable development and environmental protection.

Tourism is the preeminent salesperson for Western development, the process of planned change to raise the standard of living through technological advances and economic growth, substituting a monoculture and a single economic system for regional diversity and self-reliance. Tourism creates enclaves of Western society and development in rural and Indigenous communities that further new technologies, economic growth and free trade, and capitalist values and consumer culture. This model causes many problems. As Helena Norberg-Hodge suggests, "Today's conquistadors are 'development,' advertising, the media and tourism. . . . [This] spread of the industrial monoculture is a tragedy of many dimensions. With the destruction of each culture, we are erasing centuries of accumulated knowledge, and as diverse ethnic groups feel their identity threatened, conflict and social breakdown almost inveritably follow."[17]

In host communities tourism forms part of the total Western package of media, music, and technologies delivered to the global South. According to policy analysts Richard Barnet and John Cavanagh, these consumerized cultural products offer consumers "the illusion of being connected to cultural currents sweeping across the world, but this has little to do with the creation of a new global identification with the welfare of the whole human species and with the planet itself. . . . So far, commodity consciousness is the only awareness that has been stimulated."[18] Multilateral institutions, international aid agencies, and governments are now promoting "sustainable tourism," or "clean" development, discovering important new places to "protect." On the surface, many of the ideas appear to be credible, suggesting as they do the long-term preservation of cultural heritage sites, national parks, and other destinations. Yet this protection is offered by investors who focus on the returns a site can bring, travel companies such as hoteliers and airlines who are selling rooms and flights, and governments looking for foreign exchange and infrastructure development. This form of development, too, comes into direct conflict with the way residents have used and cared for the land for centuries. Paul Gonsalves, the Asia director of the Ecumenical Coalition on Third World Tourism (ECTWT), explains:

> Culture has repeatedly been viewed by the tourism industry in the limited sense of built heritage (historical buildings, architectural styles, archaeological sites, etc.) and cultural expression (dance, music, arts and crafts) — tending towards monumentalising culture. This takes place to the complete exclusion of the reality of which it is a part . . . everyday customs and mores, familial and social relationships, the annual cycle of planting, tending and harvesting. . . .
> Such an interpretation is at best ethnocentric and fragmentary, at worst a display of cultural insensitivity and naivete. . . . Tourism has accentuated cross-cultural stereotypes, led to mutual distrust, and accelerated cultural change (read "Westernization"). . . . Faced with threats from "development" projects such as dams, resettlement projects . . . agro-industry, displacement from traditional lands . . . [Indigenous Peoples] have clung to their culture as a basic source of identity. . . . Ironically, ethnic culture has frequently been used to promote the uniqueness of a tourism destination. Sadly, behind this transformation of culture into entertainment lies all too often a history of enslavement, enforced poverty and genocide. The commoditisation of culture for the sake of earning tourist

dollars is bad enough: it is reprehensible when it does so at the expense of a people's misery.[19]

Tourism is seen as a way to propel regional economic growth in countries, a panacea for development, especially in the global South: tourism promises jobs, economic growth, and infrastructure development. Chayant Pholphoke of Life Travels in Bangkok says that "the intent of Buddhism is to achieve nirvana. However, in Thailand tourism is supposed to achieve the same." In Cancun, Mexico, "the government explicitly decided to use tourism as a way of stimulating economic development in diverse regions of the country. While no one would point to Cancun as a desirable model of tourism development, its transformation from a fishing village with 426 residents to a major tourism center with 300,000 residents is a dramatic example of the potential for tourism to serve as a development growth pole."[20]

It is easy to understand the negative impacts of a logging company that displaces Indigenous cultures by cutting down trees or a refinery that pollutes its surroundings. Tourism is another ball game. Although many of its impacts are the same as those of other industries, tourism's enormous corporate power and long-term influence are not clearly recognized or are simply glossed over or rationalized. Tourism appears to fit into "cultural heritage" and "sustainable development" strategies since it seems that a corporation would share an interest in its communities' values and have a stake in its future. In fact, tourism is rapidly gobbling the world's remaining natural resources and displacing people from their homes. As tourists, we consider travel an inherent, economic right. Yet we are supporting the loss of jobs, subsidizing corporations, and cooperating with governments known for human rights abuses. Tourists and locals must become active citizens and make clear the connection between the corporate path of globalization and the multitude of injustices taking place under the guise of a vacation.

notes

1. Statistics from the World Tourism Organization. See *Compendium of Travel Statistics: 1989–1996* (Madrid: World Tourism Organization, Publications Unit, 1995).
2. Information compiled from various data produced in The Contribution of the World Travel & Tourism Industry to the Global Economy (Philadelphia: WEFA Group, 1989) prepared for the American Express Travel Related

Services Co., Inc. and by Wharton Econometrics, Washington, DC, The World Travel & Tourism Council, London, and the World Tourism Organization, Madrid.

3. *Clinton Administration Accomplishments: Travel and Tourism*, prepared for the White House Conference on Travel and Tourism, Washington, DC, October 1995, p. 1.

4. These figures, compiled from the World Tourism Organization, the WEFA Group, The World Travel & Tourism Council, London, and Wharton Economic Forecasting, are commonly used in tourism studies.

5. François Vellas and Lionel Bechard, *International Tourism: An Economic Perspective* (New York: St. Martin's Press, 1995). These figures are compiled from various data in the book.

6. Vellas and Bechard, *International Tourism*, p. 268.

7. IFC/World Bank, *IFC Tourism Sector Review* (Washington, DC: International Finance Corporation and the World Bank, 1995), p. 1.

8. Maggie Black, *In the Twilight Zone: Child Workers in the Hotel, Tourism and Catering Industry* (Geneva: International Labor Organization, 1995), p. 9.

9. Martin Khor, "Global Economy and the Third World," in *The Case Against the Global Economy*, Jerry Mander and Edward Goldsmith, eds. (San Francisco: Sierra Club Books, 1996), pp. 47–48.

10. Quoted from "The Trouble with Trade," in *ISEC/Ladakh Project Newsletter* 12 (Bristol, U.K., and Berkeley, CA), pp. 1, 6.

11. IFC/World Bank, *IFC Tourism Sector Review*, p. 4.

12. David Korten, *When Corporations Rule the World* (West Hartford: Kumarian Press, 1996), p. 54.

13. Alexander Goldsmith, "Seeds of Exploitation: Free Trade Zones in the Global Economy," in *The Case Against the Global Economy*, Richard Barnet and John Cavanaugh, eds. (San Francisco: Sierra Club Books, 1996), p. 267.

14. USTTA, *World Tourism at the Millennium: An Agenda for Industry, Government and Education* (Washington, DC: U.S. Department of Commerce, U.S. Travel and Tourism Administration, 1993), p. 36.

15. USTTA, *World Tourism*, p. 34.

16. Bernice Powell, telephone interview with the author, February 1997.

17. Helena Norberg-Hodge, *Ancient Futures: Learning from Ladakh* (San Francisco: Sierra Club Books, 1991), p. 3.

18. Richard Barnet and John Cavanagh, "Homogenization of Global Culture," in *The Case Against the Global Economy* (San Francisco: Sierra Club Books, 1996), p. 73. Barnet and Cavanagh also point out that "in the 1980s the environmental movement began to popularize the important idea that biological diversity is a precious global resource, that the disappearance of snail darters, gorgeous tropical birds, and African beetles impoverishes the earth and possibly threatens the survival of the human species. The cultural-environmental movement has no powerful organizations promoting its message, but it has a large, unorganized global constituency. The feeling that world culture will be degraded if diversity is lost is widely shared among artists, cultural conservatives, and nationalists. Yet these concerns are overwhelmed by

the sheer power of the global popular culture, which threatens local cultural traditions and the traditional communities from which they spring."

19. Paul Gonsalves, speech at the UNESCO-sponsored conference "Sustainable Tourism Development in World Heritage Sites—Planning for Hue, Vietnam," May 1996. (Available from ECTWT or Equations.)

20. Katrina Brandon, *Ecotourism and Conservation: A Review of Key Issues* (Washington, DC: World Bank, 1996), p. 26, quoting Magali Daltabuit, "Biosocial Impact of Tourism on Mayan Communities," paper presented at the Wenner-Gren Foundation for Anthropological Research International Symposium, Baja California Sur, Mexico, November 7, 1992.

2

the promises of tourism

Welcome to paradise! It's a place where you can relax, have fun, be waited upon. Travel promotions play on these fantasies, offering us an opportunity to purchase experiences we would not get at home, to remove us from our everyday lives and responsibilities.

Welcome to paradise—while it lasts. As villages and tribal cultures become commodified and turned into megaresorts and shopping malls, some travel agents are marketing threatened areas as places to see before they are gone. The ads gloss over the economic, environmental, and social problems in the destinations they describe, much as the tourists sites have fenced out the same realities in the host communities.

the media: spin doctors and dream weavers

The tourism industry has powerful marketing and advertising. As media critic Marshall McLuhan said, "The ads are by far the best part of any magazine or newspaper. More pain and thought, more wit and art, go into the making of an ad than into any prose feature of press or magazine. Ads are news. What is wrong with them is that they are always good news."[1]

In 1993 Pratap Rughani, an editor at the *New Internationalist* magazine, devoted an entire issue to tourism. He wrote,

Starting through dozens of tourist brochures I began to feel nau-
seous. The more I looked the less I seemed to see. Like most TV
news coverage of the Third World I was being offered images of the
South that process eighty percent of the world's population into a
quick cliche. The transformation is the opposite of "famine pornography"—this time it's fantasy-island escape. There are endless
brown and black people smiling and saying "I want to be your
friend." . . . Travel today is a commodity supporting a vast industry.
Considering the scope and economic importance of tourism there's
remarkably little analysis. Meanwhile the brochures breed. . . . The
gap opening up between this fantasy land and tourism's real impact
made me feel that brochures are in some sense obscene—"if not
vomitorial" as [another editor] put it.[2]

Tourism's corporate advertisers and marketers weave magical dreams,
illusions of paradise in the same countries that other factions of the media
and foreign aid and development authorities consider destitute. Tourists
purchase these illusions, expecting a dream and sometimes finding a
nightmare. Some of this can be attributed to culture shock and the need
to adjust to an entirely different environment. Yet most of it is a lack of
preparation and a belief in tourism industry propaganda. The perceptions
of tourism and goals of the tourism industry often conflict with those of
the host communities, governments, even tourists themselves. In the
stressful, industrialized consumer culture, the overworked and underpaid
laborers are encouraged to "get away from it all." Corporations promote
cultural homogenization at the same time they market modern resorts in
exotic locales. Travel agents present destinations as safe locations offering
a multitude of fantasy elements. They may go as far as subtly encouraging
sexual permissiveness and freedom from conventional morals. Marketers
rarely provide information that could dispel some of the unrealistic expectations tourists hold and create greater understanding between hosts and
guests. Tourists who prepare themselves for the cultural, political, economic, and environmental realities of their host destinations before they
travel experience fewer problems adapting to a temporary change in
lifestyle.

The travel industry supports biased journalism. Travel journalists benefit greatly by reporting only positive stories with little critical analysis;
they would lose not only a reputation but a job for taking a critical view
of the industry. A magazine editor who represents a major travel industry
newspaper once called me to write the lead story on environmental travel
trends for a "green" tourism magazine. He said he believed I could provide insightful criticism about ecotravel. I wrote the piece and provided

supporting resource materials. Just before press time, the editor called to say the magazine had decided the feature would not be included. Although I can't prove it, I'm sure the corporate sponsors were uncomfortable with a feature story that was not completely supportive of "green" travel. Because I challenged some of the greenwashing tactics of the eco-tourism industry, what I reported (and supported) was suppressed. There is a tremendous amount of misinformation and greenwashing taking place in the marketing of paradise.

encountering nature and other cultures ("savage paradise!")

Some of the last places on earth that have not been heavily touristed are Indigenous homelands. Marketing trends point toward the Amazon, the Himalayas, the hills of northern Thailand, tribal areas in Africa, and aboriginal areas of Canada and Australia. Travel advertisements market the residents of such destinations as people who are warm, smiling, friendly, unthreatening; who are servile and welcoming, there for the tourist's pleasure. Travel advertising says, "Come and meet the happy people, even as their paradise vanishes." This type of marketing promotes glib, racist caricatures. *Cultural Survival Quarterly* illustrated this exploitation in a cover photo: several male tourists, smiling sheepishly, cameras dangling from their necks, wear tribal garb over their Western clothes as they participate in a funeral.[3]

Consumers from the "developed" world seek solace in cultures, environments, and even the religions of disappearing cultures. Aeroperu caters to this market by advertising itself as "the new world airline" in new age magazines. A recent ad claims, "We know you're searching. For experiences. For answers. For visions of Nature's deepest secrets. We can help fulfill your request. We'll bring you close to your dream." In a recent survey, Shelley Attix, a tourism researcher, found that most new age tour companies are owned and operated by individuals who were influenced by the focus on personal growth, self-actualization, spiritual philosophies, and Eastern religions introduced to America's consciousness during the 1960s. Many undertake journeys with small groups only once or twice a year. But according to Attix, "As these spiritual trips become more like 'mass tourism,' they become less personal and harder to undertake properly."[4]

Tourism markets cultures—hula girls, wandering tribesmen, Asian mountain folk, and Native Americans. Some critics of tourism suggest that when we travel, we buy a product, a product that includes people.

Tourism offers an exciting chance (for those who can afford it) to buy or *become*, if only for a little while, a part of another culture. Indigenous rights and responsible tourism alternatives are issues that have *not* been included in economic or environmental evaluations of tourism development, although local peoples, activists, and others are now demanding serious attention from tourism developers, tourists, and politicians.

royal treatment
("a charming plantation")

Travel anywhere, at any time, and you will find glaring examples of the imbalance between so-called hosts and guests. I was traveling through the Himalayas with some local travel operators who are friends of mine when we ran into a caravan of travelers with the same company. One of the guides ran over to our van and told us they had been forced to stay up all night with a German couple who were drinking excessively. One of the pair, a middle-aged woman, had announced that she was a professional dancer and had spent the entire night making the young guides learn dances. The guides made sure the tourists were comfortable, fed, and entertained, then got up at dawn to prepare breakfast, pack everything away, and shoulder the packs, while cheerfully assisting the stumbling, aggravated tourists through another day of hangovers. This unequal treatment is one of the major selling points of tourism. Tourists are led to expect that goods and services — even human ones — are available for a nominal price, particularly in developing countries.

In Thailand I watched an elderly European male tourist pull along behind him on the beach a frightened young girl who looked no more than twelve or thirteen. It was obvious the young girl was petrified, yet there was little anyone could do to rescue her in a country that promotes the exploitation of women and children in order to cater to sex tourists. In Hong Kong and Taipei, young women dance provocatively while tourists drink, laugh, and arrange for the dancers to go back to their hotels with them. In the Amazon, renegade tour guides contract out to tourists to take them into the wilds of the rain forest to "go native." Tourists follow these guides into Indigenous villages, demand to stay with local families, eat their food, expect the locals to entertain them, and make only a token payment before they leave for the next village. The tourists are the new wandering elite, demanding royal treatment, excitement, and service from people who may not want to be part of the "travel experience."

myth: your dollars help local communities ("no more whining on paradise island")

Many tourists, unique ambassadors in the development scheme of tourism, believe their mere presence constitutes an investment in "less-developed" host destinations. In 1990 I undertook an attitudinal survey of tourists on Bali as part of my graduate research.[5] Several respondents felt that they positively contributed to the economy and served to teach the Balinese about the "outside world"; other respondents were concerned that their presence increased prices for the local people and helped to fuel the commercialism of Bali.

Investors claim that locals will receive many economic benefits for land. Once tourism takes hold, however, the price of commercial land rises to international levels, pricing local buyers out of the market. This cycle makes it easy to displace people, especially when investors buy huge areas from governments or from one local landowner at a low price. An example is the real estate and asset accumulation activity of the United States, Britain, Japan, Hong Kong, and to a lesser extent rapidly "advancing" countries like Taiwan. Investment capital from these nations buys prime real estate in the global South. Hotels are relatively "safe" investments during periods of inflation because price increases are easily passed on to the customer. TNCs and developers race to get into the hotel industry for its promise of enriching balance sheets with appreciating assets and its immediate payback.

Many of the economic arguments used to justify existing tourism are based upon the multiplier effect. This theory says that tourist expenditures ripple throughout the local economy, through transactions from laborers to local markets, benefiting the whole community. In fact, though, because of "leakages," it seems little of the money from tourism remains in the community. This is particularly true when there is a corporate chain — international hotels where transportation, food, drinks, and other products are purchased outside the country and brought in only for the tourists. According to a study of economic distribution in Tangkoko Dua Saudra, Indonesia, the benefit distribution is 47 percent to the major tour company, 44 percent to hotels, and only 7 percent to guides, of which the head reserve guard gets 20 percent. Guides and food are usually brought in from the provincial capital, so few benefits are retained at the village level.[6] In cases where leakages are up to 80 or 90 percent, that means only ten cents of each dollar will go into the community. This can be a recipe for disaster with respect to the international balance of payments for a small, underdeveloped country.

There is increasing concern about blocking these leakages and promoting local and regional goods and services to supply the tourism sector. Polly Puttallo explains: "The other side of the economic coin to leakages is known as 'linkages.' These are the ways in which the tourist industry utilizes locally produced goods and services rather than exporting them. Maximizing the linkages minimizes the leakages of foreign exchange. This process also lessens the dependence of tourism on outside factors while stimulating local economies and 'people development' and encouraging a greater sense of self-determination."[7]

Since the economic multiplier from a tourist enclave tends to be minimal, the economic payoff would be greater if the tourist resort were domestically owned. A report on tourism development in Belize pointed out that

> criticism may also arise due to the perceived socioeconomic costs of the venture. A large tourist project may have a significant impact on labor, causing workers to migrate away from traditional forms of labor. This works against a stated government policy of developing rural areas. Furthermore, the impact may only be among the unskilled labor force and freeze the socioeconomic strata. . . . Other traditional criticisms of tourism stem from a sociocultural basis. Many Belizeans fear that their country could become a "nation of busboys and waiters."[8]

Tourism is an unsustainable form of development since its instability can worsen a country's economic situation. Tourism is a seasonal, fluctuating business that can rise and fall quickly due to political changes, natural disasters (such as hurricanes), the whims of tourists, and reliance on the global economy. According to the World Wildlife Fund, "Tourism can falter when exchange rates fluctuate. How the dollar stands up to the yen or deutschmark or British pound or Mexican peso can dramatically affect the purchasing power of consumers, hence what type of foreign vacation they 'purchase.' If the dollar is weak against the pound but strong related to the peso, the tourism industry is quick to channel summer trips away from Britain and into Mexico."[9]

trends in exploitation ("you don't have to be columbus to 'discover' the caribbean")

The tourism industry follows a well-trudged corporate path that exploits people and resources around the world in the name of economic growth.

Typical Distribution of Tourism Income

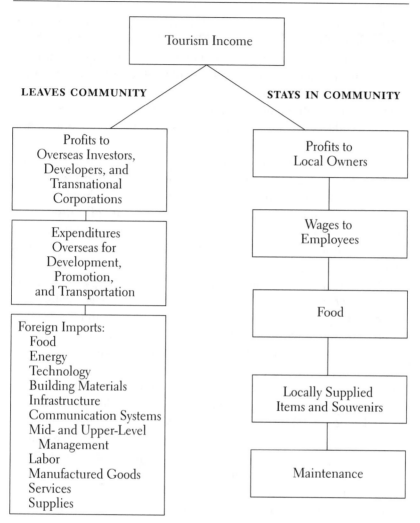

Two alarming trends are greenwashing and corporate support of countries with controversial human rights records. Greenwashing not only paints products, services, and destinations as ecofriendly but often is a screen for corporations that are actually causing great harm to the environment. The travel industry furthers human rights abuses when it collaborates with oppressive governments in the race for the almighty tourist dollar. It is difficult to imagine that tourists who are willing to shell out thousands of dollars to visit a specific country would wittingly support such atrocities. Responsible tourism and educational travel organizations are beginning to give tourists more complete information about destination communities. Some provide overviews of the country and cross-cultural training for tourists before they travel. Others offer volunteer opportunities for travelers interested in social, environmental, and economic justice. While most mainstream travel advertising continues to perpetuate misinformation, the movement to provide accurate information may push conventional marketing to do a better job. However, it is the responsibility of the individual traveler to push for the truth.

The trend toward greenwashing has its roots in anti-environmental industries. Any number of industries advertise their commitment to a clean and healthy environment. Chemical, oil, and transportation companies have designed campaigns to present polluting industries as environmental advocates. Although these companies may not be perceived as part of the tourism industry, oil and transportation are of course part of global travel. The growing popularity of pro-environmental values has been one reason these polluting industries have taken to greening up their images. The emergence of green consumerism around the 1990 Earth Day celebrations had a tremendous impact on marketing, with many old products recreated as ecofriendly, earth-saving, and biodegradable. Many of the ads for products such as biodegradable trash bags and diapers were found to contain misleading and deceptive information: the products simply were not better for the environment. But the ads still succeed.

Hotels and resorts are awarding themselves green merit points for recycling or reducing their use of plastics even as they continue to consume enormous amounts of energy, chemicals, and pesticides, particularly in the global South. Some of the greenest hotels in North America are the worst polluters in other countries, often operating without waste systems and using chemicals that are illegal in the United States. Some travel organizations donate funds to environmental protection and local health and community development programs, shifting the focus away from the environmental regulations they violate and to short-term support for local people and projects.

In 1995 the Foundation for Clean Air Progress (FCAP) was formed to represent transportation, energy, manufacturing, and agricultural groups, industries that support core operations and services for the global tourism industry. The purpose of FCAP is to lobby *against* the Clean Air Act. Burson-Martsteller, the public relations company that represents FCAP, also represented the National Smokers Alliance and its tobacco clients.[10] While making money through tourism in one area, transportation and other companies may be looking for econimic gains through the destruction of protected wilderness in another.

Sidewalk Bubblegum ©1996 Clay Butler

human rights abuses
("a carefree life!")

There are clearly misrepresentations in advertisements that promote tours to Burma (Myanmar) and other places where there are blatant human rights abuses. One tour ad says, "There's much in Burma to capture the imagination and win the heart. A thousand pagodas studding a vast plain by the muddy Irrawaddy; the reverence in the face of a child climbing the steps of the glittering Shwedagon; the delicate ballet of an Intha fisherman leg-rowing his slim vessel; and the warmth and grace of a long-suffering people. One understands how Kipling, Orwell, and many GI's building the Burma Road fell in love with this golden land." The ecotour company then notes, "We work only with the private sector in Burma. As for shaping politics, we think that the value of the two-way information flow that occurs in travel outweighs any economic benefits derived by the Burmese junta." The company goes on to advertise "The Land of the

Golden Pagoda . . . Archaeology, River Travel, Buddhist Culture, Remote Traditional Villages, Ethnic Minorities, Day Hikes. Very untouristed." The reality is that the "two-way information flow" between tourists and these locals rarely takes place. There is a trend toward "shielding" tourists: group travel is monitored by a government, the travelers given propaganda and misinformation by both the government and the tour company and escorted through their trip so they do not meet the people who are being displaced and abused.

As the tourism industry follows travelers into remote areas, it can become a support mechanism for oppressive governments, dictators, and notorious human rights abusers. Holiday Inn Worldwide, owned by the British brewing company Bass PLC, "is the cornerstone of the Chinese policy of only allowing group tours into the country."[11] The London-based Free Tibet Campaign (formerly the Tibet Support Group) claims that Holiday Inn

> has become the key to developing the exact type of tourism the Chinese authorities desire. Tour groups have to stay at government-approved hotels, usually the Holiday Inn, which explains the estimates that the revenue from this hotel alone stands at 75 percent of all foreign exchange entering Tibet. Not only are the Chinese able to extract considerably higher amounts of foreign exchange from expensive group tours, but can tightly control their itineraries, contact with Tibetans and movements more closely. . . . Holiday Inn is also subject to the volatile fluctuations of tourist numbers during the demonstrations. For example, of June 1993, after the anti-Chinese protests earlier in the year and the arrest of tour guide Gendun Rinchen, the occupancy rate fell to only 24 percent. The Holiday Inn, therefore, has a vested interest in promoting the situation as "normal" alongside the Chinese authorities, despite what may be happening in reality.[12]

Some of the largest tour corporations with the most cheerful images, those you would believe have the best interests of children at heart, are blatant examples of labor exploitation. The National Labor Committee (NLC) claims that Disney exploits workers in countries in the global South. Child workers are often underpaid, work long shifts, and in unsafe conditions. In a memo, *Setting the Record Straight/The Real Disney*, that was sent to Disney executives, NLC wrote:

> On December 17, 1996, an NBC *Dateline* undercover investigation aired which delivered another almost fatal blow to Disney's claim

to set high human rights standards for its offshore contractors, which are then, supposedly, rigorously monitored. In what *Dateline* called "the story you haven't heard—children making toys for children, for your children," its investigators revealed children "many as young as 13 years old" toiling long hours behind the "barbed wire and prison like walls of toy factories" in Indonesia and China. . . . [Some underage workers making the toys] were paid just 21 cents per hour, which is already well below subsistence levels. . . . Another impression which struck the *Dateline* team—especially in factories outside of Jakarta—was how isolated and vulnerable the young workers were. Who could they turn to for help? . . . China's Xiangjiang Province—where Disney is a major producer—shocked several of the *Dateline* team who felt as if they had somehow stumbled into the middle ages. "Here, all-night factories churn out one of every two toys sold in America. Here more than a million migrant female workers eat, sleep and work in factory compounds for just over a dollar a day." **That's 13 cents an hour.** [emphasis in original][13]

The handful of chief executives running the multinational corporations and the tourists blindly buying their products are far removed from the realities of the people who work for them. The economic gap between the CEOs of travel corporations and people in host communities is as wide as if not wider than those in any other industry.

governments chasing tourism rainbows ("a british colonial beach resort")

The tourism industry relies heavily on the cooperation, attentiveness, and performance of governments, while governments rely heavily on the economic benefits of tourism. Governments are responsible for providing safety from both political and natural forces and a modern infrastructure, the most expensive part of which may be an international airport. Many airports built in the global South since the 1980s have been financed largely by foreign governments and international aid agencies, though the host countries bear the cost of maintaining them. Expensive roads, sewers, electricity, communications, and medical facilities are also part of the tourism industry's requirements. These amenities rarely benefit locals, who may live in poverty alongside the

Western-style accommodations. Yet the locals have to finance the facilities, including the special tourist police, and rely upon a seasonal tourist economy and a fickle industry.

Economic competition has created conflicts at many levels. Governments compete with one another for the travel industry's business, offering foreign investors capital cost incentives (free land, provision of infrastructure, allowances for duty-free importation of building materials, equipment), operating incentives (tax holidays, tax credits on interest payments, accelerated depreciation allowances), and investment guarantees (for repatriation of invested capital, profits, dividends, interest and expatriate salaries, availability of foreign exchange, and exchange rates). Many governments overlook environmental guidelines and accountability as well. Increased economic competition has created internal conflicts within communities, as individuals and families vie with one another for economic benefits or struggle to maintain their lands and protect the environment.

There are thousands of "lessons learned" from communities that have received few benefits from tourism. Yet communities, governments, and investors continue with haphazard planning and growth despite the costs. A report from the U.S. Agency for International Development (USAID) discusses this worldwide phenomenon:

> Many African governments have national tourist boards that promote tourism in their countries through external marketing and public relations. In some countries, they also have responsibility for establishing standards for ground operators. Tourist boards are not noted for their concern for the environmental impact of tourism. Rarely do their marketing plans consider the impact large numbers of tourists may have on the tourist attractions they are marketing. Their mandate is simply to attract tourists, and for the most part, the more arrivals the better. Clearly their marketing efforts are not well coordinated with planning and resource management ministries of governments.[14]

It would be naive to assume that tourism development does not have strong political implications. Government commitment and investment can rarely be justified by economic advantages. According to Asian tourism analyst Linda Richter, "Socialist nations see in tourism a means of improving the international press while rightist regimes tend to encourage luxury tourism and convey a sense of capitalism rather than of more ascetic virtues."[15]

the power of corporations
("we unite the world")

Countries in the global South are not the only ones affected politically by tourism. In the United States, especially in Alaska and Hawaii, Indigenous people must confront the political repercussions of the rapid growth of tourism. Craig Chatman, a Native Hawaiian who has helped organize his community to take over operations of a state park primarily for local use, has seen how the political pressure to usurp Native lands for tourism has drastically affected local people. According to Chatman,

> Indigenous Peoples do not own their own tourism and culture. The big travel corporations have always treated Natives like "wind up the Hawaiian and let him play music." We are an Indigenous zoo and I take tremendous offense to that. All of our money is going to major corporations. As Indigenous Peoples our culture is all we have and the powers that be have exploited it. We Indigenous Peoples must take that back and show that local communities are not consumptive, but sustainable, and tourism should be too.[16]

Corporate greed is a concept far from the values of most traditional and rural cultures. From the Amazon to the Arctic, tribal people value their lands for the common good. But subsistence lifestyles and traditional economies are considered inefficient and outdated in a culture that promotes economic growth, free trade, consumerism, consumptive technologies, and exploitation of natural resources. Global economic practices are completely at odds with subsistence economies. "Because the products of subsistence activities are not controlled by market conditions and commercial profits nor are they subject to government taxes, it is impossible to say how much these products cost or what they're worth. This feature of the subsistence economy leads bureaucrats to dismiss its importance and makes governments unwilling to strengthen it."[17]

In his book *In the Absence of the Sacred: The Failure of Technology and the Survival of Indian Nations*, Jerry Mander argues that "corporate-controlled fantasies" promote manufactured culture and destinations. The message they hope to convey is that the corporations are working in our best interests and will be responsible for creating our fantasy futures. Mander warns that the trend toward remaking communities into repackaged forms of themselves and re-creating environments that belong somewhere else is symptomatic of our society's disconnection from the earth and nature. Our tendency to consume these created fantasies, the manufactured environment and culture, will result in "disorientation and madness . . . and the obsessive need to attempt to re-create nature and life."[18] The disconnection from nature contributes to the loss of a sense of stewardship for the land. The commodification of cultures and environments dilutes any sense of responsibility for the earth and distances us from social and environmental injustices. Tourists are well-trained superconsumers who have become so removed from reality, from nature, that purchasing stuffed animals that represent endangered species or t-shirts that feature a rain forest design has replaced true action to stop illegal wildlife trafficking or prevent clear-cutting. By paying for a replicated version of a threatened part of nature, the consumer is perpetrating the fantasy that he or she has somehow contributed to its preservation.

globalization and monocultures ("a place filled with warm friendly people")

Respect for local tastes and cultural differences greatly complicates global marketing campaigns. Corporate marketers promote the globalized consumer culture in order to publicize their names and sell their products with the same advertisements around the world. Tourists are "trained" to seek out names they recognize. Franchises and other corporate cultural "clones" appeal to consumers because they are familiar. On the one hand, tourism advertising creates exotic fantasies; on the other, it turns cultures into replicated, Westernized tourist enclaves. Travel corporations often make locals dress in uniforms so that everyone looks the same. Accommodations are basically the same, and the food is the same. Everything is Westernized. The world's diverse languages are not needed in an English-speaking destination. The entertainment industry, the media, and other corporations have been the source of cultural cloning that tourism brings into local communities. The transnational sounds and images choke off traditional music and arts and create a homogenized culture that reflects Western corporate values and priorities.

Tourist corridors throughout the United States have followed the same development path. The corporate takeover is evident along the major roads from New York to Vermont. Locally owned, mom-and-pop gas stations, restaurants, and shops have been replaced by Exxon, Denny's, and Wal-Mart. As public funds are used to finance infrastructure in rural areas, these corporations follow along, colonizing the communities along the transport routes to tour destinations. These corporations put mom and pop out of business, and ultimately locals become service employees rather than business owners.

tourism's truths and realities ("el conquistador: the ultimate resort!")

Author Jamaica Kincaid has captured the dominant philosphy of the tourism industry. "[you] needn't let that slightly funny feeling you have from time to time about exploitation, oppression, domination develop into full-fledged unease, discomfort; you could ruin your holiday."[19] Some tourists are becoming much more savvy consumers and are taking their local concerns and activism along with them on holidays. In the long run, the corporations that choose to greenwash, misinform, and promote vanishing cultures are undercutting their own viability and credibility. Sponsoring misinformation campaigns via marketing information and the majority of travel journalism is fraudulent and undermines basic democracy. Supporting corporations that exploit women, children, workers, and the environment ultimately threatens us all.

Changes are coming not because tourism advertising and marketing are becoming more conscientious and less exploitative but because people are demanding it. As one Native Hawaiian responsible tourism group states, "Crass commercialism, massive overdevelopment and institutionalized racism limit [the tourist's] ability to connect with the 'paradise' promised by tourism advertising. We demand ethical business practices from the tourism industry. . . . Our material poverty is not 'exotic,' certainly not to us. Images used in advertising should be fair and honest and represent our realities."[20]

As Pratap Rughani says, "If we can discard these manufactured dreams we're more likely to be able to change the tourism industry from below. Travel is a strong human urge. For me it's about hope. It's the prospect of cross-cultural communication; an exploration of self and other."[21] Travel can educate tourists about other places and peoples; it can also help them better understand their own culture and society. In an age where we are overwhelmed with images, symbols, information, and misinformation, travel can be an important way for us to communicate directly with one another. No computer, travel brochure, or television ad can ever replace that. To do that, locals must participate not as objects or dependents on tourism for their economies but as shapers of their own cultures with the right to maintain their own privacy and limits.

notes

1. Marshall McLuhan, *Understanding Media: The Extensions of Man* (New York: McGraw-Hill, 1964), from the new CD ROM series by Paul Benedetti and Nancy DeHart, *On McLuhan: Forward Through the Rear View Mirror* (Cambridge: MIT Press, 1996).

2. Pratap Rughani, "From This Month's Editor," *New Internationalist* 245 (1993), p. 1.

3. For back issues on tourism, contact *Cultural Survival Quarterly*, 46 Brattle Street, Cambridge, MA 02138.

4. See Shelley Attix, *U.S. Based New Age Spiritual Tour Operators* (Albuquerque: University of New Mexico, 1996). Attix, a Ph.D. candidate, undertook the survey, which includes new age tour operators in the United States offering shamanistic experiences, spiritual experiences, vision quests, and trips to sacred sites. Attix claims that while the tour operators can offer a basic spiritual or cultural orientation, "they can never claim to offer an authentic spiritual 'experience'; it would be false advertising." Attix points to a "considerable lack of awareness among the tour groups surveyed as to the protocols followed by local Indigenous Peoples when visiting their traditional sacred sites. Many of the companies have no local contacts in the communities they visit, or relationships with Indigenous elders" and therefore do not understand the protocols or preparations, what Attix refers to as "basic spiritual manners" required to visit important cultural and religious sites. "Many of these places are used daily by local people and are not simply historical sites with no contemporary value; they are not places that should be available for the wealthy consumer who can afford to displace locals for a chance to take photos." Yet thousands of individuals seeking spiritual journeys are not only nudging the locals out but are perpetuating cultural taboos in the process.

5. Deborah McLaren, "Earthwise Travel: Socially and Ecologically Responsible Tourism—A Global Analysis" M.A. thesis, Institute for Social Ecology, Goddard College, 1991.

6. Katrina Brandon, *Ecotourism and Conservation: A Review of Key Issues* (Washington, DC: World Bank, 1996), p. 11.

7. Polly Pattullo, *Last Resorts: The Cost of Tourism in the Caribbean* (London: Cassell, 1996), p. 39.

8. M. Cleverdon and C. Edwards, "Tourism Strategies for Transnationals in Belize," in *Annals of Tourism Research* (Elmsford: Pergamon Press, 1982), pp. 528–529.

9. Elizabeth Boo, *Ecotourism: The Potentials and Pitfalls* (Washington, DC: World Wildlife Fund, 1989), p. 12.

10. David Helvarg, "Perception Is Reality: Greenwashing Puts the Best Public Face on Corporate Irresponsibility," in *E: The Environmental Magazine*, November-December 1996, p. 40.

11. Susan Newell, "Holiday Inn: China's Profiteering Partner," *Tibet News* (London), Spring 1996, p. 20.

12. Newell, "Holiday Inn," p. 20.
13. Charles Kernaghan, *Setting the Record Straight/The Real Disney in Burma, Haiti, Indonesia, China* (Disney Memo: Separating Fact from Fiction), National Labor Committee, New York, January 17, 1997, pp. 9–10. The memo cited a December 17, 1996, NBC *Dateline* report, "Toy Story" by Stone Phillips. Transcripts are available from Burrell's Transcripts, PO Box 7, Livingston, NJ 07039-0007.
14. USAID, *Ecotourism: A Viable Alternative for Sustainable Management of Natural Resources in Africa*, report prepared by International Resources Group for the U.S. Agency for International Development, Bureau of Africa, 1992, p. 34.
15. Linda K. Richter, *The Politics of Tourism in Asia* (Honolulu: University of Hawaii Press, 1989), pp. 4–5.
16. Craig Chatman, telephone interview with the author, January 18, 1997.
17. Geoffrey Wall, "Planning the Rate of Social Change: Bali, Indonesia," paper presented at the Tourism and Socio-Cultural Change Conference, Trinidad and Tobago, 1990, p. 56.
18. Jerry Mander, *In the Absence of the Sacred: The Failure of Technology and the Survival of Indian Nations* (San Francisco: Sierra Club Books, 1991), p. 158.
19. Jamaica Kincaid, *A Small Place* (New York: Penguin Books, 1988), p. 10.
20. Hawaii Ecumenical Coalition on Tourism, *Responsible Tourism: A Hawaiian Point of View* (Kapa'a: Hawaii Ecumenical Coalition on Tourism, 1996.
21. Rughani, "From This Month's Editor," p. 1.

3

guests and hosts: disillusioned with paradise

The terms "hosts" and "guests" are used broadly throughout the travel industry to imply a congenial invitation between people of roughly equal stature. In reality, "hosts" are local people who often have little say about their role. "Guests" are actually consumers with the economic power to purchase "rights" and "services"; they are not invited by local people.

A honeymooning British couple in Bali expressed their displeasure when they found themselves at an isolated hotel on an artificial beach along with crowds of similar foreign tourists. The honeymooners had paid almost $7,000 for what they expected to be two weeks in paradise. Their lack of planning not only left them disappointed in their own accommodations but kept them at a distance from any real Balinese culture. As they explained to me, "The hotel is nice, the food is good, but it's all quite contrived. We are far away from anything interesting. We feel we are prisoners of our hotel. When we want to go to another beach we have to take the expensive cabbies provided by our hotel. Since we've already paid for all of our food and lodging at our hotel, we can't afford to visit anywhere else. We had no idea that everywhere we go we'd be attacked by people trying to sell us things. You think they really have it that bad here to have to be so aggressive? Bali seems like it would be quite a nice place for these people to make a living."

That tourists can afford to travel to a "host" community and buy the most expensive accommodations and food creates not only an imbalanced relationship but also an imbalanced perception. The tourist's everyday reality of work and responsibilities is not apparent to a person in a rural community on the other side of the world. The local who sees a carefree vacationer with an incredible amount of money is not likely to think of the tourist as a worker. And it is the rare tourist who wants to engage the locals in serious discussions about issues such as poverty, homelessness, and violence. Even if someone wanted to, the inherent inequality of the situation would create an artificiality and distance. Locals have no context in which to understand that guests must pay substantially more for shelter, food, and other necessities in their home countries. It is hard for locals to grasp that one reason the tourists are in the destination community is because it provides an unusual, short-term break from the tourists' real world.

There is an important paradox in tourism. Its inherent contradiction is that it must lure consumers away from home by implying that a tour is a rare chance to visit unique peoples and environments. But once tourists start invading, a version of the original culture of the destination is co-opted by the tourist industry and supplants the more complex, organic original. This development model reflects the colonialism that is still firmly in place in Western thought.

The consumer culture that tourism brings with it often promotes what Helena Norberg-Hodge calls the "psychological pressure to modernize,"[1] as locals begin to feel inadequate compared to the tourist consumer culture and psychologically compelled to reject what they see as their own poor culture. The tourist consumer culture creates a homogenization of culture, or a consumer monoculture.

the business of selling paradise: commodifying cultures

On Koh Samui, Thailand, developers protect choice beachfront property by building high walls along an access road. Directly across the road, isolated from the seaside resorts, is a service village built in a mosquito-infested swamp and piled high with mountains of tourist trash. Tourists' clothing, laundered by the locals, hangs like flags from lines strung up around the swamp. The village is somewhat obstructed by trees so that tourists quickly driving past on their way to paradise are not confronted with the dismal living conditions of the locals. As the destination site grows, so does the service city, with the rapid migration of people looking for jobs that require few skills.

A steady increase of tourists puts pressure on the urban infrastructure, particularly existing transport networks. An expanding tourist population means increased competition with local people for the use of the infrastructure (transportation, potable water). The stress created by these problems further alienates local people. Tourism is often seasonal, which can also strain both infrastructure and the local citizens' stamina. In crowded tourist communities on the island of Koh Samui, small trucks are the only means of local transportation. At the height of the tourist season, as many as thirty-five people with assorted luggage, livestock, and groceries are crushed into the fourteen-passenger trucks. It may be a brief, frustrating experience for a tourist who can recall it later with humor. For the people of Koh Samui, it is a permanent feature of daily life.

local people: performing for the tourist dollar

Yet local people do not present *themselves* realistically either. Governments in the global South try to sweep aside evidence of problems such as violence and pollution that might make guests uncomfortable. Local people must compete for tourist dollars and sometimes exploit each other or their cultures and environments for short-term economic benefits. This is especially true when locals market their history, ceremonies, religion, and culture.

Many local people are simply identifying and selling any community resources they think tourists might buy, sometimes fabricating performances and ceremonies they believe tourists will pay to see. In doing so they are prostituting their identities and manufacturing themselves as tourist attractions. Some are genuinely looking for ways to improve their economic situations. Others believe it's okay to allow tourists into their villages if there are restrictions and limitations regarding behavior and photography. Some want money. Others genuinely want to teach spiritual lessons. Yet not all of these individual activities are sanctioned by their communities and have caused conflicts between families and communities. For example, in the United States, several individuals offer participation in religious ceremonies such as visits to sweat lodges and vision quests, believing that non-Natives will benefit from a greater respect for the earth and sensing that these seekers are desperately in need of spirituality. According to Native American elders and leaders who are organizing to protect their spiritual beliefs from co-optation, Indian people do not "sell" their spirituality; they consider the idea extremely sacrilegious. Traditional Native American spiritual practices do not include conversion of non-Native peoples. Prominent Native organizations consider this practice to be one of the worst problems facing Native Americans today.

While some Native groups have taken measures to oppose the exploitation of Indigenous culture and spirituality, there is a growing demand by consumers who believe it is their basic right to buy anything as long as they have the means to do so. The Indigenous–non-Indigenous relationship may continue to be one of exploitation, no matter how well intended, because of global economic forces, multinational corporations, and technological development aimed to complete the eradication of Indigenous knowledge and livelihoods. According to some Native teachers, corporate practices ensure that not one wildlife reserve, wilderness, or Indigenous culture will survive in the global market economy.

A case in Ecuador illustrates how misperceptions by both tourists and locals persist. An ecotourism program in the community of Rio Blanco promotes small-scale development and community control of resources and decisionmaking. The project is operated communally by member families and expected about 300 visitors in 1996. Rio Blanco was founded in the early 1970s by Quichua migrants from the Andean foothills and relies mainly on cash-crop farming. Researcher David Schaller reports that

> community members rarely spend time in the primary forest, although tourists spend most of their time there with few believing commercial agriculture is the mainstay of the community's economy. Tourists also reported being confused and upset by the cultural program which they felt was not authentic. Not all community members indicated a connection between tourism development and forest preservation. While many community members reported they would rather increase tourism than agriculture, nearly half intended to clear more forest for cultivation.[2]

Tourists visiting Rio Blanco clearly have preconceived ideas about Indigenous Peoples living in the rain forest. They fail to see that the community is agrarian and does not rely on or have knowledge of forest resources. It depends on outside economic factors: export agriculture and manufactured cultural tourism. Neither tourists nor locals understand the global forces transforming their lives, and there appears to be no mechanism for educating either hosts or guests to evaluate their own roles and the circumstances that are bringing about disillusion on all sides.

A journalist wrote about his vacation to a Native American reservation in Arizona, where he stayed in a tepee, learned some handicrafts, and visited powwows and casinos. He referred to traditional clothing as "costumes." He had hoped he would camp within an Indian commu-

Traditional activities in commonly used open space become tourist "experiences" which make locals uncomfortable. Tourists sometimes profit by photographing open space activities and selling the photos to be used as postcards or books.

nity so he could observe daily life, but his tepee site was far from any village. Although the tour operator had arranged for him to stay on the Fort McDowell Indian Reservation, he had no contact with its tribal members, instead visiting other reservations. Even so, he ended the article by stating he was sure he'd "learned a lot about the Indians" (*Washington Post*, January 28, 1996, p. E11). Bernadine Boyd, vice president of the Fort McDowell Tribal Council told me, "We don't live in tepees here — maybe he was reading very old literature. We're a small reservation with only 2,400 acres. If someone wants to get to know us, they could do that by contacting our offices."

The article is typical of how mainstream media present Native Americans. It is clear that the writer did not consider that certain tribes might not want him on their lands or may have restrictions regarding tourists. Although he was curious about why he did not spend time on the reservations, he never looked into it. He had hoped to be in a traditional village in order to observe the lifestyles of the community. Had the journalist actually realized his dreams, he might have been surprised to find himself in low-income housing listening to barking dogs all night.

Many tourists seem unaware that simply being observed by someone can be uncomfortable and disruptive. Most tourists would feel strange if visitors to their community took photographs of them walking down the street or buying milk at the neighborhood market. It is even stranger in a community that values open space (communally shared outdoor areas such as yards, rivers and lakes, or forests) for daily activities, work, and relationships. Although the journalist touched upon the loss of land and culture, he did not delve into the issues, nor did he mention poverty and unemployment, both of which are rampant on Native reservations.

keeping cultures locked in the past

Silvio Santosa, a tourism activist in Bali, described a syndrome he calls "Tarzan and Columbus in Ubud":

> [The tourists] come to Bali, dreaming of becoming the second Tarzan or third Columbus. They look for places where there is no other white person (politely they ask for a place where there are no other tourists), although they booked their air tickets at an ordinary tourist agency, [arrive] with a regular tourist visa, and visit Bali's tourist offices for free tourist maps. They always say they are not like tourists and they don't like other tourists. . . . You may have a chance to listen to their oral science fictions in the restaurants.[3]

Many travelers have preconceived, myopic notions about other cultures. Travel journalism that idealizes Native peoples creates high expectations, and tourists (as well as journalists) are usually disappointed with the realities: people who wear western clothing, own their own businesses, and deal with tough social issues. Idealizing cultures keeps them locked in the past and sometimes creates conflicts between hosts and guests. It undermines all attempts to understand the realities of modern Indigenous Peoples.

Dharamsala, India, is the home-in-exile for the Dalai Lama and a Tibetan refugee community. The village is full of travelers from the global North seeking spiritual enlightenment or simply passing through on their way to the Himalayas. The Buddhist temple is a center for the community: every day Tibetans gather there for spiritual teaching, upkeep of the temples, and other tasks that have brought them together for hundreds of years. Children cry, locals in the back rows chat and make jokes, while others hustle about preparing things. Several times during my visits, I heard the angry comments of visitors that "these Tibetans are disrespectful at their own ceremonies." The tourist's ideal-

ization of the sacredness of the ceremony conflicted with the practical-
ity of the Tibetans, whose temples are integrated into their daily routines.
Some visitors are unaware that this is truly Tibetan religion. Tjokorde
Raka Kerthyasa, a Balinese artist, explained to me that "the ceremonies
in Bali (and probably all religious ceremonies in the world) are not commercial performances. They are part of our daily life. Because our ceremonies are unique and appear so spectacular, visitors from all over the
world come to visit and witness them. This can have a negative impact
during the ceremonies, as intrusive distractions can create difficulties and
misunderstanding for both the Balinese and the visitors." Tourist demands
for "authenticity" may indeed prompt locals to alter their practices to
ensure that tourists are satisfied and continue to come and spend money.

I have heard travelers declare that Indigenous and other ethnic people
were not "real" because they wore Western clothes or were trained in both
Western and traditional ways. They fail to consider that people living in
tourist destinations are dealing with the onslaught of tourists, consumerism,
and exploitation of their cultures.

elusive "authenticity"

Tourism is artificial in many ways. "Authenticity" is elusive when one is
part of a travel elite, an alien invader with no common history, no shared
responsibilities, no ties whatsoever to the local people and culture. And
local people rarely have an opportunity to learn who the tourists really
are. Tourism sets up a one-sided view of travelers and a creates a "tourist"
personality that encourages irresponsible and even unethical conduct.
Tourism is a magnifying lens of consumer culture; the focus is constantly
on spending money. Since tourists often believe they "help" local communities, they have established a paternalistic attitude toward the locals.
"Authenticity" can hardly be found in such a fabricated and unequal
guest-host situation.

Tourism could provide a chance for visitors to discuss with locals issues
that affect them: consumerism, employment and unemployment, homelessness, widespread psychological ills, isolationism, environmental
blight, urbanization, drugs, racism, women's issues, education, stress, the
lack of extended families and community support, violence, the gap
between rich and poor. There are few opportunities to talk about how the
world is on a course of overconsumption that is eroding the planet's natural resources and displacing millions. But more important is the potential to exchange through listening and learning. Travel can counter the

myths and harmful activities of the global North while supporting local efforts and creating useful cross-border organizing with those in the global South who share similar concerns. It could also be a way to work together toward the common good of the planet.

the economic power to buy: shopping for culture

Tourist Trick or Treat

The restaurant left nothing to chance,
promised not just the best in local food and wine
but the "cream" also of their traditional song, music and dance.

At the appointed hour air-conditioned coaches and taxis
arrived to disgorge their cargo of tourist-diners
eager to sample this exotic feast of cuisine and culture.

Halfway through dinner to the raucous fanfare of
castanets and congas, they spilled on stage:
the singers and dancers with serviette smiles
as beguiling as their garlands of plastic flowers.

Singing and screeching their swiveling hips in mock-raffia skirts,
serving a dish specially concocted for tourists neither Asian
    nor Polynesian,
it was a cultural desecration that turned all the wine in our glasses
    into vinegar.[4]

In his ode to tourism, lawyer Cecil Rajendra exemplifies how manufactured culture has turned tourist destinations into stereotypes difficult to dispel. Few tourists have escaped a welcome lei, a smiling greeting committee of native women bearing necklaces and drinks, a welcome-to-Jamaica shot of rum, or other such cultural concoctions. Yet manufactured culture goes beyond the initial welcome to include almost all tourist experiences—dining, excursions, and entertainment. Millions of tourists routinely experience their entire vacations through the lens of counterfeit culture.

Tjokorde Raka Kerthyasa told me, "Some tourists and visitors who know nothing (or do not want to know) about the meaning and purpose of our customs and religious practices attend ceremonies just for the sake of taking pictures to prove they have been on a holiday." In the small Balinese arts village of Ubud, dances are performed for tourists, but their evolution has been unusual. Rather than being manufactured and approved by the tourism industry, the performances are the work of the community. Members of the community, many of whom have gained international recognition, perform dances and music in the courtyard of the Ubud Palace. Kerthyasa argues that the tourist performances can reinforce local culture: "more (young) people are willing to learn techniques from the old masters." Community members, especially family and friends of the performers, watch along with the tourists. Balinese children see their parents weave hypnotic visual and musical compositions. Although these performances, too, are contrived, they are an accepted form of traditional ceremonies and dances that the community has decided to share with tourists. Yet those who oppose this form of tourism suggest that the pressure not to change may prevent normal progress, even if it serves to benefit the local people.

purchasing the "other." Tour agents sell "the Other"— ethnic cultures that are not part of the dominant, Eurocentric consumer culture. Writer and professor bell hooks, who speaks widely on issues of race, class, and gender, believes the market offers a commodity culture that exploits conventional thinking about race and gender. According to hooks, the current wave of "imperialist nostalgia," where people mourn the passing of what they themselves have transformed and destroyed,

> takes the form of reenacting and reritualizing in different ways the imperialistic colonizing journey as narrative fantasy of power and desire of seduction by the Other. . . . The desire to make contact with those bodies deemed Other, with no apparent will to dominate, assuages the guilt of the past, even takes the form of a defiant gesture where one denies accountability and historical connection. Most importantly, it establishes a contemporary narrative where the suffering imposed by structures of domination on those designated Other is deflected by an emphasis on seduction and longing where the desire is not to make the Other over in one's image, but to become the Other.[5]

In our homogeneous society, the longing for the primitive is expressed in tourists' projections of another culture. The tourism industry exploits destination cultures as exotic, bohemian, mystical, culturally rich, glorified societies. As hooks says, "Masses of young people dissatisfied by U.S. imperialism . . . afflicted by the post-modern malaise of alienation, no sense of grounding, no redemptive identity, can be manipulated by cultural strategies that offer Otherness as appeasement, particularly through commodification."[6] Travel to rural and Indigenous cultures is increasing at a rate never seen before as the world becomes globalized and we lose our cultural identities and ties with community.

In our capitalistic society, individual power lies in economic strength, not in who we are or what we contribute as a whole to our communities. This is the central difference between Western societies and those societies where individuals think of themselves as part of their larger community and tradition. Industrialization has fostered human isolation. People feel lonely and detached even within cities filled with millions of people. Westerners are indeed prime customers for cultural purchases since we are living examples of commodities ourselves. How much we make, what we can afford to buy and do, the level of education we can pay for, and our monetary assets classify us and constitute our individuality. As imperialism persists throughout our own society we, the modern colonialists of the new tourism frontier, culturally isolated consumers that we are, seek out opportunities to purchase a fleeting, exciting, intense encounter with the Other. But many Indigenous Peoples claim tourism is just a form of cultural voyeurism, allowing the curious to glimpse Native cultures.

As hooks explains, simply by expressing the desire for "intimate" contact with other cultures, foreigners do not remove the politics of racial domination. She encourages us to recognize that purchasing an experience with another culture is a form of racism and that "mutual recognition of racism, its impact both on those who are dominated and those who dominate, is the only standpoint that makes possible an encounter between races that is not based on denial and fantasy."[7]

macabre forms of tourism. One of the most disturbing phenomena in Bali is the commercialization of cremation ceremonies. After a water ritual at a village stream, private rites are performed. The people then proceed through the village together, bearing the body to the cremation site in a huge bull built out of wood and paper and beautifully decorated. Women dressed in colorful, hand-dyed skirts carry sculpted fruit offerings.

A death is now big news on Bali, and many tour operators sell tickets to the cremation ceremonies. Signs in front of the tour offices urge, "Don't Leave the Island Until You See the Big Cremation—Get Tickets Here." Once a death is announced, local agents contract minivans and buses to deliver tourists to the destination village. Since ceremonies take place in public areas with village participation, there is little locals can do to keep tourists from joining the procession to the cremation site.

We offer you

Don't leave bali
Before you see
a big cremation

on   : 19-4-91
depart : 11.00. am
price : 10.000 Rp

please book here !

PT NOMINASI
CHANDRA
WISATA.

Herick

DEBORAH MCLAREN, BALI, INDONESIA

Even death and funeral rites have become commodified for tourism in Bali where enterprising businesses begin arranging tourist vans and selling tickets as soon as they hear someone is dying.

Local people are crowded out by aggressive tourists who want photos. In fact fences must be built around the cremation sites to keep the tourists out of the immediate area. Along the fence tourists crowd shoulder to shoulder, pointing their cameras at the burning funeral pyre. They are careful not to get any other tourists in their photographs. Their photos are calculated to show friends back home that they were one of the special few to see such an exotic religious ceremony—although as many as 200 tourists may be on hand. A British tourist who witnessed the activities at a ceremony remarked, "It was an amazing experience, but I felt bad for the local people carrying the body when two motorcycles joined the procession. These tourists rode up wearing only their swim suits, waving bottles of beer and having a great time. I was embarrassed to be there."

Even tragedies become an excuse for travel as information about other countries becomes more accessible through the media. Tourism becomes all the more bizarre. In Somalia vagabond tourists come to view the famine and human tragedy. A U.S. newspaper reported,

The heightened world focus on Somalia has also brought a new and unwelcome group of visitors, whom the relief workers refer to as "misery tourists." Many of them are young backpackers traveling around Africa who hitch rides on a relief plane from Nairobi to Somalia for no other reason than to see the suffering. Some claim to be freelance writers; others have cameras and say they would like to sell pictures of the dying back in the West. But most are simply voyeurs of misery, global rubberneckers who are putting themselves and legitimate foreign reporters at considerable risk.[8]

Some locals view tourists as a possible means of help, while others react with pain to having their suffering photographed and documented. The *Wall Street Journal* recently reported that Westerners by the thousands visit Papua New Guinea for safaris. For about $10,000 per person, they go to tribal war zones to gawk at humans marketed as warring cannibals:

> Visitors jet in and out of villages, snap a few photos, and are back at their resorts in time for a five-course dinner. . . . Critics call it one of the most macabre forms of tourism today. Though casualties in the tribal skirmishes are rare, the battles can be brutal and bloody—something that human-rights groups say shouldn't be exploited for tourism. "It's voyeuristic," says Barbara Gehrels, a manager at Survival International, a London-based group that monitors tourism of Indigenous peoples. Paul Taylor, who heads the Asia history program at the Smithsonian Institution, says it is worse. "You're subsidizing warfare," he says, "You're almost encouraging it."[9]

Not all tourists visiting these areas know about the cannibal tours and are appalled to learn about it. Tour operators argue that "tribal tourism isn't exploiting anyone, in part because the tribes are accepting money. 'We want the people to maintain their culture,' [a tour operator] says, 'That's what sells Papua New Guinea.'"[10] Tour operators to Irian Jaya, Indonesia, where tourists participate in funeral processions, also claim the income keeps the locals happy and the tourists coming. Yet the local people are concerned about the loss of cultural artifacts, burial gifts, and icons, which the tourists take home as souvenirs. One visibly shaken woman told me, "They took my mother's image [a wood carving]; they have stolen her soul."

elvis batiks: manufactured tourism culture. There is radical resistance to manufactured tourism in many Indigenous societies that have become tourist destinations. In Hawaii, where tourism is now the dominant industry, the commodification of island culture has been so complete that the image that probably comes to mind when you think of the atoll is smiling, friendly women in grass skirts who cater to relaxing tourists.

Haunani Kay Trask is a Native Hawaiian activist who is keenly aware of the cultural costs tourism imposes through commodification and remanufacturing. Trask charges that an entire Indigenous culture has been successfully commodified, the culture deformed to the point of prostitution. Prostitution in this context "refer(s) to the entire institution which defines a woman . . . as an object of degraded and victimized sexual value for use and exchange through the medium of money."[11] Trask describes how *haoles*, or white tourists, have stereotyped and commodified Hawaii:

> The commodification of Hawaiian culture includes a marketing of Native values and practices, on *haole* terms. (After all, a prostitute is only as good as her income-producing talents.) These talents, in terms, are the "hula," the generosity, "aloha" of our people, the "u'i" or youthful beauty of our men and women, and the continuing allure of our lands and waters. Tourism converts all of these into profits. Hula dancers wear clown-like make up, don costumes from a mix of Polynesian cultures and behave in a smutty manner, rather than in a powerfully erotic manner. The distance between the smutty and the erotic is precisely the difference between western culture and Hawaiian culture. In the hotel version of the hula, the sacredness of the dance has disappeared, and been replaced with an ornamental hoax. . . . Needless to say, Hawaiians don't participate (in manufactured tourism), and didn't participate in such things before the advent of *haoles* in the islands.[12]

Tourists often do not comprehend that other people *live* in a place; that they are born, grow up, and die there; that it is their home. Perhaps it is the anonymous nature of tourism—the lack of obiligation, the likelihood tourists will never visit the community again—combined with the self-righteousness of purchasing power that allows tourists to deny their part in the exploitation and to participate in activities they would consider repulsive at home. For example, tourists have a reputation for wearing inappropriate clothing. Travel advertising encourages tourists to be free and easy in their dress as much as everything else. One famous photograph shows two Muslim women on a beach, even their heads completely covered, curiously glancing at a bikini-clad tourist in repose on the sand. It is a striking image of the contrast between women of two cultures. Yet the tourist has the economic clout to do as she pleases, even when it challenges every moral standard of the culture she visits.

Corporations have long been in the business of manufacturing traditional arts and crafts, clothing, and other cultural "artifacts," crowding out those made by traditional craftspeople. The goods are mass-produced, eliminating the local artist and using cheap labor outside of the country. It is not uncommon to find vases from China, t-shirts from the United States, and belts from Guatemala in souvenir shops in any country. Traditional arts and crafts are highly commercialized under the power of tourism. For instance, in Malaysia and Indonesia the fine art of batik, a dye and wax process that creates beautiful prints on natural fiber, is now mass-produced on synthetic materials in hundreds of factories throughout Southeast Asia, and traditional designs have been replaced by pop art and Elvis Presley. Traditional crafts like bamboo art and reed weaving are marketed in a wide range of new applications: as beer mugs, candle holders, and coffee and tea sets. Over the past few years, many Latin American Indigenous handicrafts have taken on the Guatemalan style of bright colors and simple patterns. In Otavalo, Ecuador, most of the products sold in Indian markets are faux Guatemalan. The Kunas of Panama recently began to sew cartoon characters into their hand-layered textile motifs, or *molés*, replacing traditional designs and animal figures. This may be simply a change in culture, but it is a change that stems directly from tourist demand.

However, to counter the exploitation of traditional arts, local craftspeople in many destinations have organized cooperatives to ensure that they are not taken over by outside industry. Women artists throughout Java and Bali, for example, have joined handicraft cooperatives. Yet there is increasing concern from local businesspeople and artists as the doors of free trade swing open that these cooperatives are in competition with each other. This is the case in Otavalo, where weavers have destroyed competitors' looms.

Along the highways of the desert southwest in the United States, billboards beckon tourists to stop at "Real Indian Trading Posts." Kachina dolls and sacred pipes are sold alongside rubber tomahawks. In the Black Hills of the Dakotas, where a non-Native-owned tourism industry pulls in $1 million annually, tourists dress up like Indians to get their pictures taken beside an "Indian chief." More than 2.5 million tourists each year stop by to see Mount Rushmore and visit the local Indian population.[13] Few Indians have been able to adapt to the new conditions; they are viewed only as relics.

Tourism scholar Dean MacCannell says, "When an ethnic group begins to sell itself . . . as an ethnic attraction, it ceases to evolve naturally. The group members begin to think of themselves . . . as living representatives of an authentic way of life. Suddenly any change in life style is not a mere question of practical utility but a weighty question which has economic and political implications for the entire group."[14] Staged authenticity places tremendous constraints on a community. It is difficult not to let the demands of tourists outweigh a community's own power and lifestyle. Concerning her own community, Haunani Kay Trask warns, "Tourism deforms the culture so much that many young Hawaiian children grow up thinking that our culture is the *haole* interpretation of culture—to dance the hula is to dance for tourists . . . and if you smile real nice, some *haole* is going to take you out."[15] Any argument for rethinking tourism must be made by the community itself, as should the effort to balance economic interests with critical protection for its people and culture.

The Hopi Nation may be one of the last holdouts. Signs warn tourists not to take photographs or wander past designated areas. When Anne Coyner, an intern working on the Navajo reservation, traveled to Hopi with a Navajo friend to visit an acquaintance, they were stopped before they could enter the residential section of the village. A Hopi woman told her, "It may not seem like there are a lot of people around, but you would be surprised to learn how many eyes are watching." Each village makes its own decision about tourists, but the overarching sentiment is obvious with so many tourist warning signs appearing on the reservation. Ten of twelve villages have closed their kachina dances to the non-Indian public. The Hopis enforce tourist guidelines, including dress codes, and a camera or artist's sketch will be confiscated. Tourist inquiries to the tribal office receive the following reply: "Hiking and off-road travel is strictly prohibited because of the disregard for the sanctity of our sacred religious shrines by past visitors. The Hopi Tribe does not publish a schedule of traditional ceremonial activities as these are religious events that are not staged for the entertainment of tourists. Such publicity would be disrespectful of their very spiritual nature."[16] So far, the Hopis are determined to keep tourists at a distance and keep their culture intact; they have taken strong stands against all types of development that would influence their culture.

political disruption and travel boycotts

In 1989, just after the Tiananmen Square massacre in Beijing, tours were canceled and there was a quick and massive exodus of tourists who were both frightened and protesting Chinese government actions. According to the *Wall Street Journal*, China lost an estimated $1 billion in its projected tourism income for 1989.[17] The United States and other countries issued advisories against travel to China and invoked other sanctions. But within a few months the Chinese government invited hundreds of foreign travel agents to bring tourists back, explaining that things were back to normal. The tourists who entered China after the massacre often got preferential treatment. Political unrest can change the dynamics of tourism quickly, with the resulting damage affecting all levels of the host country's economy. Tourism as a mode of economic development is "sustainable" only in a stable political environment and in a political economy with healthy international relations. Small businesses and the people who operate the open-air economy of tourism must find their own ways to survive. The Chinese government made substantial efforts to promote international tourism after the Tiananmen Square rebellion, upgrading transportation, creating a historical theme park, and forming the Chinese Scientific Exploration Association to promote scientific tours.

The effects of foreign tourism boycotts on governments and people are difficult to determine, although they are a powerful tool to make countries toe the line of economic liberalization. Because local economies become so dependent upon foreign ones, many of the immediate effects are on the local businesses, whether they are part of the open-air economy or the official economy. In the case of China, many Chinese activists believed that economic sanctions should be increased against the state but that tourism should continue. A Chinese living in the United States said, "We don't want China to be closed off from the rest of the world." It is a catch-22 for conscientious tourists: not to travel in China censures the Chinese government's actions while isolating China's people from outside contact.

Burmese solidarity campaigns around the world have responded quite differently by calling a boycott of the "Visit Myanmar (Burma) 1997" campaign, sponsored by the country's repressive government. A representative of the Free Burma Coalition I spoke with warns, "Tourist dollars do not benefit the people of Burma; the tourism promotion is an effort by the government simply to gain currency while carrying out gross human rights abuses on its citizens." Over twenty Burma support groups around the world have warned tourists, the travel industry, and the media that visiting Burma under its brutal military regime supports human rights abuses and only furthers economic trade and political ties without solving injustice.

expanding corporate influence on the global economy

Often transnational corporations hold a monopoly on an entire segment of the tourism industry. One example is hospitality firms, especially lodging corporations, which have entered into tourism through the hotel development business. Firms build hotels and then sell them to investment groups, perhaps becoming involved as investors themselves, primarily to ensure that they will be able to secure the contract for the long-term management of that property. Most such firms thus become management contract organizations. They also continue their monopoly by franchising. They use others' capital to fuel growth and ensure cash flow. Cash-rich European and Asian transnationals, for instance, have been acquiring U.S. hotel company assets to demonstrate growth and aggressiveness in their capital markets. This pattern is not limited to the United States, however: it is occurring throughout the world. It is not unusual to see cash-rich firms from different nations pooling their resources to acquire assets in another nation.

Transnational corporations often undermine the efforts of local businesses. A recent study of the most visible members of the informal economy in Acapulco—street vendors—suggests that "street vendors are generally less informal than is . . . assumed. They have licenses, sell in broad daylight and have open relationships with formal sector suppliers. . . . Domestic tourists buy from lower-priced street vendors in response to the higher prices charged by formal establishments. Paradoxically, hotel owners are those most opposed to allowing street vendors on the beach."[18]

Some governments regard tourism as a political bridge among nations and cooperative alliances between countries have been employed through organizations like the Association of Southeast Asian Nations (ASEAN). Other organizations, such as the World Bank, USAID, the International Monetary Fund, UNESCO, and others, have been instrumental in providing aid for tourism and have some impact on tourism global policy. Specific international tourism organizations such as the World Tourism Organization and the Caribbean Tourism Association have been indirectly involved in international policymaking. Government and national organizations exist to monitor ecological concerns. The World Commission on Environment and Development, however, recently noted that the nation-state is inadequate for dealing with global threats to the ecosphere. Unfortunately, in almost every instance "the most common measure of development is an economic indicator—GNP per capita."[19]

government euphoria

As tourism becomes a major force in global trade, governments are eager to attract it, often at any cost. Tourism initially appears to be a "win-win" situation, according to many governments. The government is pleased since they have facilitated an entire industry and stimulated economic growth. The investor and developer must be pleased; after all, haven't they concocted a wonderful fantasy where tourist dollars are handed over with happy smiles? Tourists must be delighted as well, because their very presence gives local people new jobs; they are now part of the global economic market. And the local people must be happy, since they are reaping the economic benefits of increased tourism.

The reality is that many governments and states do not have adequate tourism ministries or departments, nor adequately trained people to staff and manage them. The few young people moving into new tourism jobs within the government have in many cases been taught since elementary school that their country will suffer without tourism. An enormous amount of secondary school educational materials in the global South, especially targeting dropouts, are designed and funded by tourism corporations and international development institutions.[20]

Many governments regard tourism as a way to increase foreign exchange earnings and subsequently improve their balance of payments. The expansion of the service sector and subsequent generation of employment attracts investment capital for infrastructure development. Policymakers and business leaders rarely consider the social, ecological, and political factors of tourism. Eventually, the expanding infrastructure, operations, and security require governments to tax the tourism sector. Often the government becomes dependent on the tourism sector for direct and indirect revenue (income from sales taxes, airport departure taxes, corporate taxes), especially as more sustainable, traditional economic activities such as fishing and farming are displaced to make room for tourism development. Yet this reliance upon the tourism sector, combined with the heavy investments governments must make in building and maintaining the tourism industry, make it even more dependent and vulnerable to the global economic market and increasingly competitive tourist products and services. The Center for Responsible Tourism reports that "even government leaders need to guard against overly optimistic conclusions based only on arrivals and expenditures and promotion costs (of tourism). The more difficult social measures will require more subtle analysis."[21]

Countries around the world are including tourism in their national action plans and national environmental plans. Bhutan was one of the first, and many other Asian and Latin American countries have followed suit. Since tourism has become the second highest income earner in developing countries (behind oil),[22] this seems a reasonable part of good planning. Yet these plans are often in the same euphoric stage that communities find themselves in, embracing tourism and "ecotourism" development haphazardly, with little integrated planning.

In India, the government suddenly made tourism a major part of its

New developments in paradise: tourism, McDonald's restaurants, and construction in Guam.

action plan, hoping to make it the country's highest net earner of foreign exchange. The tourism minister announced a package of measures to increase the number of tourist arrivals from 1.5 million to 5 million in five years and to double the amount of hotel rooms in three years. But the tourism minister's projections did

> not disguise the transfer of power that he envisaged for the industry, from the public to the private sector, from blanket to intensive development of specific "routes" and "destinations" around the country. The National Action Plan [NAP] was designed to herald the arrival of resort tourism, and attract the free-spending visitors whom India had never been able to draw. . . . So far, the only beneficiaries of the NAP and its accompanying baggage have been the hoteliers, who have been building with enthusiasm, using loans guaranteed by the Tourism Finance Corporation (TFIC) and benefitting from tax breaks provided by the government.[23]

As of 1995 there were more than 35,000 hotel rooms planned and fifteen special tourism areas (STAs) designed with financial incentives to encourage private investment in hotels, infrastructure and other tourist facilities.

> The sites were selected on the basis of consultations between hoteliers and tourism departments, both state and central. And here the

problems began. . . . Had tourism officials solicited the views of the Ministry of Environment and Forests before conferring STA status on Orissa's Marine Drive, then considerable embarrassment and expense could have been spared. The result has been red faces in the state's Tourism Department and the unwelcome discovery that local sentiment cannot be ignored, even to the convenience of large hoteliers. . . . [Sixty hoteliers applied for permits to build and] the plan would entail the felling of a reserved forest, encroachment on the Balukhanda black buck sanctuary and the subsequent exposure of the coast's agriculture to the shifting sands and cycles that had prompted the British to plant the forest in the first place.[24]

People in fifty villages in the area learned about the expansive project and feared that the forest's destruction would turn their fertile land into sand and threaten their way of life. Local people further opposed "the culture of affluence." The state tourism minister, also a resort owner, applied for land in the proposed area to build his own hotel. "And so arose one of the nation's first tourism-related political movements, as *panchayat* [community] leaders mobilized thousands of locals . . . which resulted in a broad-based coalition which three times thwarted the attempts of Chief Minister Biju Patnaik to have the state's forests deregulated."[25]

In 1995 I visited India on an environmental fellowship that focused on private enterprise and biodiversity protection through ecotourism. I met with several state tourism ministers to discuss ecotourism development; all of them told me that tourism was not involved with any other governmental sectors and that they did not see a need for integrated planning. Although they had a tremendous interest in and expectations for increasing international tourism, these tourists represented a mere 10 percent of all tourists to some states. And most tourism ministers could not adequately track income from tourism, where it came from and where it went.

moving to equity

In the 1970s the World Bank claimed that tourism would be a beneficial opportunity for development in Cuzco, Peru. Local studies of the region report that "tourism has not translated into an employment boom for the region. When you look at the number who are actually employed by the tourist industry . . . it really turns out to be just a few. . . . Out of 280,000 economically active persons in the region, only 6,000 (slightly more than two percent) are directly or indirectly employed by the tourism industry."[26] Commercial enterprises such as high-rise hotels rarely use the local population as the management system. Foreigners usually fill mid- and upper management positions. Locals are employed mostly in service-level positions (as maids, waiters, bellhops, transportation help), and there are infrequent opportunities to advance into management positions. Only rarely, when they already have extensive education and language skills, are locals sent abroad for management training.

The tourism industry can be merciless. When increased economic growth is the leading factor for development, conflicts and competition develop between people, between communities, and even between nations. Political systems are under pressure to provide goods and services that tourism developers, TNCs, and even their own populations desire. Market forces are determining the shape of world economic activity in general and tourism in particular. There is a need to encourage efforts to establish decentralized, locally owned projects that will ensure tourism is socially and ecologically responsible. Another need just as great is to encourage responsible and responsive research and development to support these programs.

Tourism has become the new form of colonization over the poor of the world. As one responsible tourism writer wrote, "The past decade has seen the colonization of the developing world by the tourism industry. Considering that international travel accounts for the exchange of more than $3 trillion a year, it may be safely said that tourism exerts a greater, more pervasive influence on the countries and cultures of the world than any imperial power ever has. . . . The sun never sets on the tourist empire."[27] Virginia Hadsell, founder of the Center for Responsible Tourism, recently told me that she believes there are some promising new developments. "There are more responsible travel writers and magazines. The responsible tourism movement continues to grow, and important links have been made with the travel industry. There are more local people organizing their communities and doing homestays or building modest accommodations, providing personal tours, and introducing guests to the way real people live—not the glitzy high-rise hotels, golf courses, sun, sex and sea."

People-to-people experiences that are equal, informed, and further understanding about common concerns—and joys—are the only way to avoid disillusion between "hosts" and "guests." Understand what you are "buying" when you travel, demand realistic information from the travel industry, learn about tourism's role in undermining local economies - and cultures, and support local communities and responsible tourism organizations. Investigate and boycott irresponsible tourism industries. Take action against economic liberalization and privatizing the environment. Most important, work for change in the community where you live or the one that you visit on vacation each year.

notes

1. Helena Norberg-Hodge, "The Pressure to Modernize," in Edward Goldsmith, Martin Khor, Helena Norberg-Hodge, and Vandana Shiva, *The Future of Progress: Reflections on Environment and Development* (Berkeley: International Society for Ecology and Culture, 1992), pp. 81–101.
2. David T. Schaller, "Indigenous Ecotourism: Rio Blanco, Ecuador," Ph.D. dissertation, University of Minnesota, 1996.
3. Silvio Santosa, "Bali Pathfinder" (Bali: Silvio Santosa, 1990), p. 12. Available from the Ubud Tourism Information Center.
4. Cecil Rajendra, "Tourist Trick or Treat," *Responsible Traveling*, 9(3): 4.
5. bell hooks, "Eating the Other," in *Black Looks: Race and Representation* (Boston: South End Press, 1992), p. 25.
6. hooks, "Eating," p. 25.
7. hooks, "Eating," p. 28.
8. Keith Richburg, "Pests Amid Famine," *Washington Post*, October 13, 1992, pp. E-1 and E-6.
9. Nancy Keates, "Tourists Take 'Human Safaris' in Pacific," *Wall Street Journal*, December 20, 1996, p. B-12.
10. Keates, "Tourists," p. B-12.
11. Haunani Kay Trask, *From a Native Daughter* (Monroe, ME: Common Courage Press, 1990), p. 11.
12. Trask, *Native Daughter*, p. 11.
13. These figures are from the 1996 *Visitation* statistics available from the Rapid City Convention and Visitors Bureau, Rapid City, SD, p. 29.
14. Dean MacCannell, *The Tourist: A New Theory of the Leisure Class* (New York: Shocken Books, 1989), p. 6.
15. Trask, *Native Daughter*, pp. 11–12.
16. Quoted from the standard information letter sent in response to tourists' inquiries from the Hopi Tribal Office, Kykotsmovi, AZ, 1996.
17. *Wall Street Journal*, July 31, 1989.
18. Daniel Hiernaux Nicholas and Manual Rodriguez Woog, *Tourism and Absorption of the Labor Force in Mexico* (Washington, DC: Commission for the Study of International Migration and Cooperative Economic Development, 1990), p. 16.
19. D. M. Smith, *Human Geography: A Welfare Approach* (London: Arnold, 1977), p. 47.
20. See, for example, Robert Prosser, *Tourism* (Surrey: Thomas Nelson and Sons, 1982). This text was funded by the Overseas Development Administration-UK,

an extension to the Schools Council Geography for the Young School Leaver Project, and used in the Caribbean.

21. Linda K. Richter, *The Politics of Tourism in Asia* (Honolulu: University of Hawaii Press, 1989), p. 6.
22. John Naisbitt, *Global Paradox* (New York: Avon Books, 1994), p. 170.
23. Christopher de Bellaigue, "Packaged Confusion," *India Today* (New Delhi), February 28, 1995, p. 187.
24. de Bellaigue, "Packaged Confusion," p. 189.
25. de Bellaigue, "Packaged Confusion," p. 189.
26. Rebecca Cunningham, "Peru: Tourists Flock to Cuzco," *Responsible Traveling* 14(1): 3.
27. Jim Molnar, "In an Era of Mass Travel, Tourism Becomes the New Colonial Power," *Seattle Times*, September 10, 1989, p. J-12.

4

tourism development in
the local community

imagine one morning you wake up
and walk outside to pick up the newspaper. Flash! Aliens with cameras
giggle and point at you while their children run through your yard, jump
on your car, and scream for their photos to be taken. Down the street you
notice a couple of hip young aliens returning from an early morning
swim at the beach. They stop by your church on the corner, still in their
skimpy, wet swimsuits as they wander in to watch your neighbors participate in services.

Click! Flash! The duck pond in the middle of the block has become
an overnight attraction. Suddenly 200 aliens gather around its small
shores, trampling the flowers you helped plant there last spring. The
ducks fly away. You walk down the street to the corner market to pick up
some things for lunch only to find that the market is so full of aliens that
you can't get through the aisles. One top of that, the aliens are willing to
pay incredible prices for practically anything in the store. You can't afford
to be here; quietly you slip away. What's wrong with this picture?

Tourism means turmoil for residents of tourist destinations. Social pressures—a changing local environment and economy, increasing numbers
of tourists, and the effects of media and technologies brought in to support the development—build up very quickly and change lives and cultures forever. Many changes are obvious, while others are subtle. In some
cases communities have become human zoos. For example, hill tribespeople in northern Thailand and the Masai in Kenya have herds of
trekkers and caravans of camera-toting tourists seeking them out; Karen

tribal women along the Thai-Burma border are enslaved and brought out only for tourists.

Indigenous cultures are being devastated by an invasion. At this level tourism creates its own universe, an artificial world with no place for the local population. It is a struggle for the locals just to survive. Given the almost total lack of government control, the absence of industry self-policing, and most important, the increased competition to make a profit, the tourist industry more than ever wields unprecedented power in communities.

Ladakh, fortressed above the Himalayas on the Tibetan Plateau, was virtually isolated from the West until the mid-1970s, when the Indian government, worried about border conflicts with China, built an airport and increased military presence there. Overnight the West invaded—tourists, media, technologies, pesticides, roads, and consumerism. Helena Norberg-Hodge observed the process from the beginning:

> I became aware that our [Western] culture looks infinitely more successful from the outside than we experience it on the inside. . . . With no warning, people from another world descended on Ladakh. Each day many would spend as much as a hundred dollars, an amount roughly equivalent to someone spending fifty thousand dollars a day in America. . . . Ladakhis did not realize that money played a completely different role for foreigners . . . [in Ladakh basic needs were free of charge], that back home they needed it to survive, that food, clothing, and shelter all cost money—a lot of money. Compared to these strangers, they suddenly felt poor.[1]

The psychological pressures took on many forms of cultural rejection. Begging became an increasing problem. Some farmers began to call themselves donkeys, indicating they were poor work animals next to the wealthy tourists. The tourists looked at the Ladakhis as if they were backward or primitive. When I visited Ladakh in 1990, hundreds of tourists from the Middle East were there to escape the Gulf War. Many of them told me they believed Ladakh was backward. An American woman who lived in Kuwait told me that "if the Ladakhis could understand that better resorts would attract better tourists, they might escape from this poverty."

Tourism promotes the same colonial tendencies that agricultural export companies, missionaries, and others perpetrated in earlier centuries. Colonizing is not new, but tourism development as a form of colonizing is new and growing at tremendous rates. Between 1950 and 1990, tourist arrivals grew from seven million to eighty million in the Americas; from virtually nothing to almost fifty million in East Asia and the Pacific; and from less than a half million to fourteen million in Africa.[2] The numbers are remarkable and the effects catastrophic.

sociological cycles of tourism development

Tourism's emergence in host communities follows a typical pattern. The first stage is euphoria, which is typified by the residents' race to trade everything they have (land, natural resources, autonomy, culture) for the "riches" of the global economy. Many local communities and governments are passionate in their belief that tourism is the path to all future development. The multinational tourism industry promises jobs, distinction, and outside support to the community or country.

Tourism researchers often refer to the second stage as apathy: locals begin to notice changes, such as restrictions of their traditional land use, and their initial excitement wanes as they realize few benefits. The tourism industry fashions an irresistible fantasy of jobs and money. Few communities have the knowledge or experience to see through the illusion, nor do they have the resources to plan for its problems. Tourism divides communities into those who believe it may provide some benefits and those who are opposed. There is a need at this critical moment for tools and information to help the residents analyze the situation, make informed choices, and develop strategic plans by looking at other models (including other communities that have resisted tourism or created alternatives). Yet development agencies, investors, and governments rarely provide this information, and locals seldom realize the economic and employment opportunities promised by this conventional path of development. Infrastructure for tourist use is subsidized by public funds, but the public rarely uses it. In fact prices for public transportation often increase beyond the local public's means. The locals are displaced and priced out of an international real estate market. Prostitution, alcoholism, and venereal disease increase; traditional skills are forgotten; the beautiful landscape erodes.

As the infrastructure is built, competition between hosts and guests mount. This is the third stage, when hosts become antagonistic and blame their growing problems on tourists. Competition accelerates between locals and tourists for transportation, sanitation, food security, money, space and environment, and even cultural integrity. By the time the locals have experienced the full cycle of tourism, they are too debilitated to fight back. The new infrastructure makes the region more desirable for other industries besides tourism. The urbanization facilitates migration to the area and provides corporations with a pool of cheap labor. A system is created to train locals and migrants for service jobs in tourism or as low-skilled labor for other industries.

The stratification between rich and poor, tourist and local, is fueled by the new consumer culture. Locals invariably begin to regard themselves as "poor." When a community loses its self-reliance and depends on foreign corporations for wages, necessities like food and shelter become unaffordable. The globalization of the economy transforms the local and self-sufficient (tribal, farming, hunting) community into a consumer-oriented and dependent society. Convinced that internationally manufactured goods are superior, they reject their own, locally produced goods.

Since he now relies upon an income in a monetary economy, the local cannot afford the things he once owned. He eventually drifts into the impoverished population of the service industry. In the past, as a subsistence farmer, he had agricultural skills, knew where his food came from, and was self-supporting. His family did not rely upon his income to ensure their shelter, and a fluctuating seasonal tourist market did not jeopardize his livelihood. Once considered a landowner or a farmer, he was an important member of his own community. As a bellhop or busboy, he contributes little to the community, his status declines in the new tourist society, and his descent into self-rejection begins. This pattern of economic gains and losses is not addressed in traditional accounts of tourism.

economic myths

Tourism is praised as a source of employment in host destinations. It is seen as a highly labor-intensive industry that can offer employment to the semiskilled and unskilled. In regions where there is high unemployment, tourism is said to provide moderately quick relief. In some countries that are predominantly rural with semiskilled and unskilled labor, nearly all the management personnel must come from abroad. Positions like caterers and cooks tend to be filled by foreigners; in fact expatriates may even be needed to fill a portion of the unskilled staff in this labor-intensive business. The majority of locals are left with low-wage jobs. With few management training programs, there is no escape from a life of service jobs.

Despite their history of callous indifference to employees, TNCs are still encouraged by governments who buy into the same promises of job creation. Governments lavish money on beach resorts, although recent statistics show "beach resorts account for just seventeen percent of total jobs created, despite having received the greatest share of government support."[3] The hotel industry is heralded as a job source and may benefit from official programs, yet

> contrary to the usual claims, the hotel industry is not the main source of job creation in tourism—one of the key objectives of official tourism promotion programs [in this case, in Mexico]—since its share in total direct employment is under fourteen percent. . . . Jobs in surface transportation, travel agencies, and airlines account for ten percent of total direct employment, a relatively low figure. The greatest relative job creation is in services, restaurants and bars. These account for forty percent of the total direct employment.[4]

Tourism offers temporary, low-wage jobs without long-term commitment from the industry or benefit for the community. In most of the world it's an unstable source of jobs, since tourism is inherently seasonal. Benefits common in North America or Europe are unheard of, year-round employment nonexistent. Even in hazardous construction work, there are no contracts, no insurance, no benefits. Many hotel and resort construction sites are labor camps, with entire families living in makeshift shanties.

A tourism activist in Hawaii relates what tourism developers promised and what really happened:

> [The developer] promised 6,500 jobs when he was collecting permits to build. What he seems to be saying these days is something not so promising. The tourist "industry" is the lowest paying major industry in the state; most of it paying minimum wage. And when there is a slump, you are sent home: "don't call us, we'll call you." Often the lay-off is far too short a time to collect unemployment, but long enough to consume any meager savings one might have. Even these jobs will go to those with the skills and education needed to function in the resort scene.[5]

Many hotels and restaurants in tourist sites are foreign-owned, so the dollar spent by the tourist almost inevitably does not stay where it is spent. A great deal of the cost of a vacation is transportation, the means of which are overwhelmingly controlled by the countries from which tourists come. Moreover, the growing tendency for the same company to own a "chain" of travel businesses, or "corporate alliances," opens up a further channel for ensuring that the minimum amount of money is received by the host community or country. In many countries it is difficult to determine the links in the "chain." In the United States, Disney's director of public affairs, Bill Warren, told me that "corporate alliances are part of the package. We have alliances with all the major hotel chains, any number of airlines, cab companies. . . . It literally gets into the thousands."

human rights, migration, and displacement

Tourism development has fostered human rights abuses and supported oppressive governments. In some cases the locals are seen as a nuisance to tourists, and the military patrols areas to keep the local vendors away. In countries with records of human rights abuses, the government has displaced local people and sometimes even enslaved them as workers to build hotels and other sites. Government tourism officials prevent locals from having contact with tourists.

In addition, many people in destination communities around the world are fighting for their own land rights. It is usually the poorest and most underrepresented and marginalized who are simply fighting for their right to have a place to live. Some atrocious examples were reported in the media in 1996 when the president of the Philippines ordered entire shantytowns be torn down to "beautify" the area for international development meetings. Most fights over land rights are directly in conflict with governments and private investors.

The group Tourism Concern supports global campaigns to protest displacement of people caused by tourism in Burma, Indonesia, and Kenya. Burma, a country with an atrocious human rights record, "celebrated" 1996–1997 as the Year of the Tourist to promote economic growth and investment in the country. However, many of Burma's tourist sites were constructed by forced "voluntary labor." In Pagan 5,200 people who lived in villages among ancient pagodas were given two weeks to move and were allowed no compensation or anywhere to go. Now Pagan and its pagodas welcome tourists in peace and quiet while its people live on bare, parched earth with little shelter.

The island of Lombok in Indonesia has gained popularity with international tourists, and the Indonesian government is demolishing homes to make way for tourism development. "Hundreds of thousands of people in the Third World are facing malnutrition and starvation, not because of famine or war, but because they have lost access to the land and resources that could sustain them. It's happening because their governments are pursuing the tourist dollar, and need more room to develop the industry."[6]

Several tourist developments in Africa displaced the traditional population; people who had lived there for thousands of years, cultures that made a living on sparse lands and existed only because of access to the area's natural resources. The Sarova Shaba Hotel in Kenya was built in the Shaba National Reserve for tourists:

A spring provides fresh water for the hotel, and, where it emerges through the rocks outside the lobby, it cascades over a series of waterfalls into a pool below, where fish swim and water lilies cover the surface. The bedrooms of the hotel are situated around the enormous swimming pool. This was once the watering-hole used by the local Samburu and provides the only pure water in the region. . . . The Samburu are now confined to arid land devoid of grass. . . . The plight of the Samburu is desperate. Their cattle are dying from drought conditions and loss of access to water, and now the people are faced with starvation.[7]

In Kidepo Valley National Park in Uganda, the situation for another tribe is even more dire:

Before the creation of the park, this was the land of the Ik, a viable hunter-gatherer society who hunted game and gathered wild vegetables, roots and berries as they moved. . . . During their annual nomadic cycle which took them into parts of Sudan and northern Kenya, they would collect honey. . . . They had little impact on wildlife because they only killed for their own consumption. . . . When the valley was declared a national park, the Ik were forcibly evicted without warning. The Ugandan National Park Act is very strict and rigid and does not allow for any form of local utilization. The tourists who visit Kidepo are mainly Europeans and North Americans who come on hunting safaris. The Ik are now confined to an inhospitable area of steep mountain slopes, which was previously only a temporary resting place during their travels. Unable to successfully follow their previous lifestyle, they attempted dryland farming as a means of subsistence, but the land is fragile and subject to frequent and prolonged droughts and their crops fail repeatedly.[8]

How about a golf vacation? What could possibly be a problem? Golfers might find it hard to believe that the construction of golf courses around the world has become a factor in displacement of people. According to Chee Yoke Ling, director of the World Anti-Golf Movement,

> Uncontrolled proliferation of golf courses world-wide is directly threatening people and natural resources. While the last few years have witnessed increased discussions on sustainable development, golf development is becoming one of the most unsustainable and damaging activities to people and the environment. The 25,000 golf courses world-wide cover an area as large as Belgium and the business of building them is one of the fastest growing land developments in the world. Golf developers in Third World countries pay golf architects like Jack Nicklaus US$1 million for designing a course, far more than the compensation paid to the people it displaces.[9]

The United States is not immune to this phenomenon, as Native Hawaiians have been displaced by the popularity of golf. "In 1986, Yasuo Yasodo, a Japanese national, bought the 1,200 acres that our homes were on for the last 30–50 years. We are Keiki O Ka'Aina (children of the land), yet we were evicted, our cattle stolen and killed, our houses bulldozed and our lives ruined just so a Japanese foreign national could build this lavish golf course complex. We are now gone from the land we loved, it is too late for us, but we plead with the Japanese government . . . do not let [these] investors come to Hawaii and terrorize us."[10] Ling reports that the Keiki O Ka'Aina plea has gone unheeded: "Japan's national airline, JAL, has recently obtained approval to build a huge resort with a 27-hole golf course, a restaurant, 100 units of private lodges and 1,440 luxury houses on 1,500 acres of agricultural land and 800 archaeological sites on the west coast of Hawaii. Traditional burial grounds are also included in the area. . . . Displacement even takes place for the ancestors of the local Hawaiian residents."[11]

How about a cruise? The staff always seemed happy on the *Love Boat*. About fifty cruise ships sail from U.S. ports, although most are registered in countries like Panama to avoid U.S. laws that protect cruise ship employees, "seafarers." The community of people from the global South who live and work on cruise ships often put up with squalid conditions and little pay. According to the Center for Seafarers Rights, "500–700 workers are on each ship, typically from 30–40 different poor, underdeveloped nations, working and living side by side. Most workers have no written contract, work 12–14 hours a day, often get no day off for an entire year, live in cramped, unsanitary rooms deep in the bowels of the ship, are fed poorly and are only paid a few hundred dollars a month."[12]

So many cruise ships pay inadequate attention to safety standards that numerous fires have resulted in recent years, triggering an investigation by the National Transportation Safety Board. Responsible tourism organizations suggest investigating the living and working conditions of seafarers. This is difficult to do, since "guests" are not allowed to visit the living areas of employees. But "When approached with dignity and understanding they will often open up and let you know what life aboard the ship is really like. Most crew members will appreciate your genuine effort to get to know them as human beings."[13]

loss of traditional culture

Tourism researcher and scholar Valene Smith writes that the seasonal nature of tourism "may leave hotels empty, carriers and tour operators idle, and employees jobless. . . . Individuals who are tied to tourism experience either 'feast or famine.'"[14] The local people do not often experience the "feast." Most of the accommodations at a tourist destination are owned by outsiders. The service-level jobs local people fill do not provide enough benefits ever to call them "feasts." Most of the millions of people who make up the world's tourism labor do not have job security, health care, or a minimum wage. Outside of countries in the global North, few countries have labor unions. In some countries, unions are created by the corporations and not the workers, effectively controlling any protests from labor.

But the local people are familiar with the "famine." Enticed by the promise of jobs that will allow them into a monetary economy, they often give up work on land and a subsistence lifestyle to become dependent upon a monetary economic lifestyle when they migrate to the service cities. Because of the seasonal nature of tourism, local workers make meager wages during the high season and virtually nothing during the off-season. This is clearly not a feast-or-famine situation; instead, it is more a "low-maintenance-or-famine" one. While in the Westernized view "subsistence" has negative connotations, to those from other cultures "subsistence" can mean success. Yet tourism displacement forces people from lands that offer a subsistence lifestyle.

Multiple problems arise from the clash between Western, technological cultures and traditional cultures. Like other large TNCs, corporations in tourism are rapidly replacing workers with computers, particularly

in communications and financial services, doing away with phone operators and bank tellers, for example. Travel hospitality suppliers, travel
agencies, air transportation, travel vendors, corporate travel managers,
and megacorporations that provide travel technologies and integrators
are areas that increasingly promote new technologies. Other technologies that support tourism, such as tools and machines used in water and
sewage, construction, agriculture, and transportation, also downsize job
opportunities for locals. Other, more subtle problems arise from the culture clash. Friction often comes about over the concept of time. Tourists
from the high-tech world expect locals to move faster, sometimes ridi-
culing or in other ways degrading employees who may be ill trained for
their jobs and may have only rudimentary skills in foreign languages. As
time-saving technologies are introduced, life gets faster for both local people and tourists. Workers are exploited by tourists and the industry who
consider their economic value only, not their time or the toll that introduced technologies have created. As Norberg-Hodge explains, the shift
from traditional lifestyles to a technological world "represents a shift from
ethical values that encourage an empathetic and compassionate relationship with all that lives toward a value-free 'objectivity' that has no ethical foundation."[15]

Norberg-Hodge questions the reasons for traditional Western development paths: "I believe that the most important breakdown of traditional
societies is the *psychological* pressure to modernize."[16] Traditional societies were self-sufficient before "development" came along. Introduced
development ideologies, technologies, and outside influences, such as
tourists and the media, represent consumerism's most exaggerated fea-
tures. "Development" undermines self-esteem and eventually becomes
"essential." It is easy to understand how people, especially the young, are
blinded by the promise of capitalism when their exposure to Western
culture is so narrow: the media and movie stars or travelers who seem to
be rich, unburdened by jobs or responsibilities. The "psychological
pressures to modernize" and the promise of economic gain are potent
rationalizations for tourism development.

All forms of development are based on economics. "The word 'development' presupposes agents that engineer change: changes in the natural environment, changes in social structures, changes in production
patterns, etc. These changes are supposed to generate improvements in
the quality of life of the people involved. . . . The idea of development is
very much a concept from the North. Its roots go back to at least the
period of Enlightenment. . . . It was then that the early colonial powers
started to establish administrative systems to rule and control huge regions
in the South."[17]

The very language of development, terms like "First World," "Third World," and "less-developed countries," reinforce the Western biases about poverty. The U.S. Agency for International Development was established to "develop" the rest of the world in its own image, one that holds capitalism and economic growth as a central value. In addition, interconnected agencies and pacts such as the International Monetary Fund (IMF), the World Bank, and GATT were established to form a structure to manipulate world trade. They are directing the world's development processes: liberalizing environmental, labor, and economic barriers and developing the world infrastructure in order to reach natural resources. The road to progress has had only one path, one that has proven ineffective and incongruous for most of humanity.

transnational corporations

Even in the United States, where TNCs are common, their effect is palpable. The wide reach of TNCs is shown in Hawaii, where families who acquired wealth through plantation agriculture now own tourism. These families are selling and leasing land to TNCs for hotel and resort development. Real estate prices escalate and locals rarely can afford to buy their own lands, although public support is required to provide services and infrastructure. The future of Hawaii is determined by TNCs that are interested only in investment, overseas corporate boards who base decisions on speculation and sometimes money laundering. Development is no longer grounded in community well-being or used to promote local self-reliance and decisionmaking.

The TNCs are becoming more influential, powerful, and political. They have a strong hold on the tourism industry, creating the "need" to go on vacation and for the development of destination communities. According to Matthew Rothschild,

> In today's world, the single most important economic actor is the [TNC]. A few hundred of these giant companies, based in the U.S., Europe and Japan, affect the lives of people all across the globe. They influence what we eat and wear, and at what price; how we make our living, and at what wage level; where we reside, and whether we—or they—own the land we live on. They poison our water, pollute our air and contaminate our food. They corrupt our governments and ally with those who deprive us of our rights. [TNCs] play such a role because they have enormous power, and

because they are interested not in our well-being, but in the making of profit.[18]

Critics argue that developing countries form the majority of the world's population and should be free and equal participants in the shaping of world development. However, TNCs maintain a hold over international relations. Although such global institutions as the United Nations exist to rectify conflict among nations, TNCs have historically rejected the decisions of international organizations that don't suit them. Many of these corporations also control the world's resources and wealth. These superpowers have vast economic and military clout and are ultimately able to control countries in the global South.

TNC hotelier conglomerates often operate through consortium-type organizations, spreading control to additional companies rather than into the community. In many cases TNCs are franchises. Name recognition for a hotel chain or product is promoted by franchising, and the financial arrangements are attractive to both franchisee and franchiser. By forming global travel partnerships (affiliations among credit card companies, banks, transportation, travel agencies, hoteliers) and unfettered by the free trade laws of any nation, TNCs have solidified their dominance of world tourism. This, along with the amalgamation of frequent-user programs by hospitality and travel firms (for instance, frequent-flyer programs that merge with hotel and car rental programs), suggests that the marketing alliance effort will continue and that community control and benefits will be suppressed.

TNCs with few tourism development restrictions are responsible for problems of much of the infrastructure in destinations in the global South. Land planning and layout design by these global corporations often interferes with environment and local traditions. This type of development has not met with a favorable reaction in many communities. Tourism researcher Linda K. Richter has written that at "tropical paradise" destinations in Indonesia "some Balinese are fighting to retake some measure of control over the tourism industry before it pollutes the very culture so many others came to experience. . . . Accommodations like the traditional *losmen* allow guests to stay in small-scale labor intensive accommodations that range in scale from modest hostels to luxury inns. These units are ecologically far more compatible with the environment than the high rise, high import, high energy five star hotels that the World Bank helped finance."[19]

Examples of TNC control in the United States abound. Seibu Alaska, a local unit of the giant Japanese Seibu Group, owns the Alyeska ski resort in Alaska. Seibu is spending $70 million on a luxury hotel and mountain "improvements" to cater to wealthy Japanese skiers. Such developments offend many Alaskans. In Talkeetna, "a hamlet in Mt. McKinley's shadow, residents have presented petitions and staged a rally to protest a large Denali National Park visitors center [that was] proposed for their tiny town."[20]

effects of tourism development on indigenous peoples

In many places around the world, the conflicts among TNCs, governments, tourists, and Indigenous Peoples are coming to a head. Any analysis of these problems must avoid lumping all Indigenous Peoples into one ethnic group with the same set of concerns. Rather, each group should be viewed within its own set of circumstances, concepts about land use and development, and most important, according to its own right to self-determination.

Eurocentric patterns of privatizing lands are at direct odds with Indigenous concepts of land, which include strong emphasis on managing for the common good and taking responsibility for the earth. Colonization, acculturation, and industrialization have a long history of affecting virtually every Indigenous group. Vine Deloria and Clifford Lytle write about the impact on Native Americans: "Expansionist forces beyond the government's control inevitably destroyed the effort to keep the Indian and white communities apart. The increasing sophistication of American technology enabled settlement where none was thought possible so that, as the Indians were pushed farther west, they were replaced by a civilization that could not easily be dislodged, a civilization that was intimately linked to eastern industrial society."[21] Tourism continues the same human, technological, and industrial invasion of Indigenous lands. Of Hawaii, tourism activist Kaleo Patterson says,

I have seen the exploitation caused by an out-of-control global industry that has no understanding of its limits, nor responsibility or concern for the host population of a land. I can say with certainty that the majority of Hawaiians long for a better way of life, of simple respect and dignity, that today's tourism industry has systematically undermined. . . . At a place called Honokahua, a developer's excavations unearthed over 1,100 intact burial bundles, while local community groups protested in anger. It took mass demonstrations before the developer stopped. Tourism is not an

Indigenous practice; nor has it been initiated by the native Hawaiian people. Rather, tourism promotion and development has been directly controlled by those who already control wealth and power, nationally and internationally. . . . While local elites and transnational corporations benefit from tourism, native Hawaiians remain the poorest, sickest and least educated of all peoples in Hawaii. Current trends show that tourism will never benefit us.[22]

The past few decades have seen an unprecedented force to be reckoned with as Indigenous Peoples organize around issues like land rights, civil rights, and intellectual property rights. They are powerful players in developing legal structures and policies prepared by the United Nations and the World Bank. They are becoming a solid force that TNCs in the timber and oil industries must recognize and work with. Indigenous Peoples are succeeding either in resisting tourism's negative impacts or formulating creative strategies to take it over on their own terms. While many Indigenous Peoples remain fairly isolated and do not have the experience and history required to understand and deal with tourism, new international strategies and alliance-building around the issues will establish connections between those who know tourism all too well and those who are new to it.

Many tribal people resent the purchase and practice of Native cultures and religions by outsiders. These sentiments are part of a growing movement. In the 1980s the American Indian Movement (AIM) issued resolutions condemning non-Native adoption of facets of Indian spirituality. Certain writers, anthropologists, and others have been banned from Indian lands because of their exploitation of the people and their religion. American Indian groups have issued a declaration of war against non-Indian cultists, commercial profiteers, and self-styled new age shamans.

here come the tourists!

"Give me the t-shirt," the woman said to the tourist. The small village in the Amazon was almost filled with beggars. It was hard to believe that the community began its ecotourism project in 1992 in order to protect natural resources. The villagers had lost interest in the land and became enchanted by things the tourists had. Their repeated "requests" annoyed tourists. Some locals were more skilled and playful in their requests; others up-front and demanding. "They have money and many things," said the woman asking for the t-shirt. "It's no problem for tourists."

It is easy for locals to perceive tourists as incredibly wealthy. The entire tourist experience revolves around money and purchases. The community itself is being purchased. Tourists are superconsumers who bring their foreign languages and communications, strange and inappropriate clothing, and cameras into the community. In the context of a brief visit, sometimes an overnight, few real friendships are formed between tourists and locals. Tourists are eager for adventure, or at least the perfect photo opportunity. If the tourist becomes upset in the midst of the excitement, the local usually pays the price. But these strange people sometimes give away token gifts to locals, even money. This results in begging, which becomes increasingly widespread as locals begin to see themselves as "poor" and the tourists as "rich." The psychological pressure of viewing oneself as poor or backward can manifest itself in crimes not previously common in a community.

Indigenous Peoples in the Andes demand compensation for having their photographs taken, saying it's intrusive. A woman in Otavalo, Ecuador, explained to me, "We see ourselves and our children on postcards and in books. We do not benefit from having our photos taken. A foreigner does. We demand part of the profits." In some Indigenous communities, photography is taboo because it is believed to cause physical or spiritual harm to the person who is photographed. In India young children have had limbs torn from their bodies to make them more pathetic and hence "better" beggars. Adults who commit this violence often have several children who work for them. Other forms of begging sometimes found amusing by tourists offend many locals. An Indigenous leader from Panama told me, "It breaks my heart to see the young boys swimming after coins the tourist throw in the water. We spent years acquiring our rights to these lands. Now with tourism, the people here do not care about the land anymore. They just want tourist dollars."

While tourists believe they can contribute to destination communities, locals don't always agree. Money spent by budget travelers—especially backpackers—may go into the local economy. They tend to stay in cheaper hotels and eat in cheaper restaurants owned by locals and so get closer to the local culture. These young vacationers like to distinguish themselves as "travelers," not "tourists." They live by budget travel guides and often flock to the same inexpensive areas of villages and cities. But in "frontiers" like Kathmandu, Goa, and Bangkok, where a backpacking subculture has existed since it became part of the "hippie" routes in the 1960s, such travelers have a reputation for stinginess and rude, hard bargaining. In Indonesia I met a British bicyclist who was cycling around the world. He was proud that he had spent virtually no money on his trip. He lived with families that took him in every night from the road and ate

The tourists: from the locals' perspective.

ISEC/THE LADAKH PROJECT

what was offered to him by people he met along his way. He had not worked in any of the places he had visited. He was extremely happy that he had just bargained a local merchant down from the equivalent of ten cents to a penny for four pieces of bread. I thought it was rather odd that he was taking advantage of everyone he met and wouldn't even pay a fair price to a poor baker.

health issues

Tourists are often concerned about infections and illnesses they might contract while on vacation to another country—with good cause, because as tourist destinations become more urbanized, disease increases. The fear of disease can lead to declines in tourism; both Thailand and Kenya have suffered drops in tourism with the rise of AIDS. Tourists avoid parts of Africa and Asia because of malaria. Globalization has created scares about diseases and bacterial infections spread by tourists, like cholera. Even the ebola virus was believed to be transported by airplanes.

While most travelers are concerned only about their own health risks, they are responsible for the expansion of disease. Tourism carries diseases and bacteria to new areas, travelers routinely bringing home the diseases they have picked up: in the United States, virtually all of the 1,173 cases of malaria reported in 1991 were contracted overseas. The AIDS virus has spread to Europe and the Americas as tourists return to their home countries from well-known sex destinations. However, the disease tourists leave behind during the trips is rarely accounted for. An estimated 90 percent of Indigenous Peoples in the Americas died after exposure to infectious diseases imported by Europeans, and over half the groups once present in the Americas have become extinct. Millions of people in tourist destinations face health risks from tourists. AIDS is such a problem in Thailand because of tourism that hundreds, perhaps thousands of women, men, and children are dying as a result. Other sexually transmitted diseases are on the rise. Increased prostitution, alcoholism and drug addiction, displacement, and toxic and polluted environments attributed to tourism development have further contributed to a variety of health problems.

Parts of Asia and South America are now popular with a particularly lethal visitor, the drug tourist. To "go native," they find jungle guides, seek shamans, and take hallucinogenic drugs. In northern Thailand the high demand for opium among tourists has trickled down to the population at large, and many hill tribespeople have become addicts who cater to tourist demand. There is little or no treatment available to local people who become addicted. Tourists return home after a few weeks, never seeing the chaos their thrills have caused.

In Peru drug-voyeur tourists are traveling into the Amazon and bringing health problems that threaten the local population. The Urarina people have remained relatively isolated because of the remoteness of their settlements and by choice. The very reclusiveness of Urarina has contributed in large part to their reputation and served to draw this new breed of tourist. While they resisted missionaries and the culture of the colonialists, according to infectious disease physician Ritchie Witzig,

> Incursions of "foreigners" (non-Urarinas) into Urarina traditional lands are currently from river traders, loggers, colonists, oil exploration teams, and recently "drug-voyeur" tourists. . . . In the past two years, two Americans have arranged "jungle ecology tours" that include a two week trip up the Amazon and Maranon rivers, and recently the lower Chambira river. During the river tour, a "shaman" from Iquitos manufactures the sacred hallucinogenic ayahuasca (*Banisteriopsis caapi*) for the tourists to drink and "experience the jungle like natives." Finally, they arrive in Urarina

NORTH-THAILAND

POSTCARD AVAILABLE IN THAILAND

This postcard of an addicted tribesman in Thailand, a tourist souvenir, is an example of how tourism capitalizes on local drug use created, in large part, by demand from tourists.

villages to "look at the Indians" and take pictures. Right after a tour in the spring of 1995, most of the children in a village which had been visited came down with a respiratory ailment requiring antibiotics to recover. This infection was most likely supplied by these "drug-voyeur" tourists from overseas. The Urarina are alarmed at this invasion, especially as they know the tour operators are armed with weapons and take drugs, effectively mocking the Urarina religious ceremonies. The affected villages organized to write a complaint to the Peruvian Ministries of the Interior and Tourism in Iquitos, and the American Embassy in Lima, demanding that the individuals responsible be barred from their lands.[23]

Witzig believes that "ecological destruction and introduced diseases will gradually decimate" the Urarina, who "will likely need political support from outside Peru or they will join the long line of extinct cultures and peoples left behind by the ongoing colonization of this continent."[24]

The general health of people in tourist destinations is declining, and locals are the least likely to be able to afford treatment. If doctors are available, they usually serve wealthier tourists who can pay them. The claim that tourism will bring with it better health services is a myth. Tourists and locals compete for access to health care. When people are displaced, their health may be at greater risk because they have to relocate to places where it is more difficult to survive. The strain of development that accompanies tourism also destroys the environment and creates poverty and urban health problems. The lack of proper water and sewage treatment and virtually no garbage control further threaten locals. Quick-fix serums and vaccines cannot cure the real dangers to health: environmental devastation, increased urbanization, and related social ills.

women and youth at risk

Women and youth in particular are harmed by tourism and tourists. As traditional cultures are turned into service cultures, it is women who are most likely to be demeaned by the industry as prostitutes and hostesses. In some countries very young girls and boys are recruited to serve the demands of a growing global sex tourism industry and are exploited by tourist pedophiles.

The following is an excerpt from a letter sent to the German embassy in Bangkok:

> For the duration of my stay in Bangkok, I would like to hire a Thai girl. Since I do not want to return to Germany with the clap [gonorrhea] or syphilis, I would like her to be examined by a dermatologist or in a clinic. I would, therefore, be very grateful if you could give me the address of a reliable doctor or clinic. Perhaps you could also inform me of the approximate cost of an examination. Or is there even an agency in Bangkok which guarantees that its girls are healthy? Thank you very much in advance for your trouble.[25]

According to the Ecumenical Coalition on Third World Tourism (ECTWT), what is most striking about this and numerous other letters sent to official German institutions in Bangkok is "not so much the brazenness of the request itself, than the unabashed way in which it is taken for granted, that the recreation value of a holiday resort can be reduced to a mere question of the quality of brothel services."[26] In some countries prostitution tourism has become so rampant that it not only attracts the sex tourist but is drawing some travelers to the countries permanently to become sex-tour guides and experts. Referring to a well-known American engineer who moved to Thailand and started writing "prostitution guidebooks," the ECTWT warns that "when an engineer becomes a tour guide, when skilled doctors (of which Thailand has not enough) specialize in serving tourists, when business people become marriage brokers, it is obvious there is money in the sex trade. We can clearly see who profits from it, but the real question raised is what is the cost?"[27]

Tourism prostitution is legal in some Asian countries. Japanese travel agencies send participants to Taiwan and Thailand, although tours are also organized from Europe, the Middle East, and the United States. While there are supposedly restrictions on the number of prostitutes in some countries, two to three times more illegal prostitutes are working in Taipei today than those who receive licenses. Governments simply look the other way, since prostitution tourism is a lucrative business. At almost any bookstore or newsstand in Hong Kong, visitors can purchase *The Businessman's Little Black Book*, which is advertised as a compendium of essential information for the business visitor. After a few quick pages outlining how to establish a business and obtain servants in Hong Kong, the book goes into a twenty-two page section on nightlife, which begins, "Let's start with sex" and goes on to list how and where to approach Chinese women. It contains pages of colored photographs with updated telephone numbers handwritten in.

Women are not the only ones exploited. Tens of thousands of boys and girls are made prostitutes for tourists to parts of Asia, Africa, and the Middle East. Sri Lanka and the Philippines attract the highest rates of pedophiles. "The majority of pedophiles come to Sri Lanka on the recommendation of one guide book or another. One such guide, referring to the Philippines, says 'Manila is the world's ultimate paradise for gays including pedophiles.' After discussing various places where plenty of young boys can be found, this guide suggests that a good way of procuring a partner is to 'hang around various schools as students are leaving' in order to presumably to pick them up as they walk home." [28] End Child Prostitution in Asian Tourism (ECPAT) estimates there are 80,000 child prostitutes in Thailand, 60,000 in the Philippines, 30–40,000 in India, and 15,000 in Sri Lanka."[29] Through ECPAT's efforts more child sex offenders can now be prosecuted in their home countries.

More than 130 countries, 500 NGO representatives, and 1,000 concerned individuals and the media participated in the World Congress Against Commercial Sexual Exploitation of Children in 1996 in Stockholm. UNICEF, a chief participant, reported that more than one million children a year are forced into prostitution, sold for sexual purposes, or used in pornography, and many are trafficked across national borders. According to Broken Bud, a prostitution tourism watch organization in the United States, the reason for such high numbers of exploited children is that "their own families, driven to desperation by crushing poverty—often caused by the economic injustice of first world countries—sell them, yes, sell their children."[30]

Children are at risk from tourism in many ways. Children and youth go to tourist centers because they can beg, deliver drugs to tourists, prostitute themselves, or get the low-skill jobs typical of hotels and restaurants. Even young people who live with their families are attracted to the potential economic benefits and the lifestyles of the travelers. A traveler-youth culture has appeared in every city around the world. The young people, often out of poverty or desperation, are lured by the consumer culture and reject their own cultures as primitive compared to what they perceive to be the travelers' culture. The result is the youth are drawn away from their families, communities, and more traditional activities to spend time with tourists. They become isolated from their families and often have few options other than making a meager living from tourists.

Child labor is extremely common within the tourism industry. Young children work in hotels, restaurants, clubs, and bars, the open-air economy of the tourism industry that is not formally recognized. In Ecuador I met a little boy who was ten years old and "managed" a hotel. He had been stolen from his mother in a market when he was three. Abandoned by a "foster" mother when he was nine, the boy had managed to find employment in the tourism sector. He worked for a family who owned a hotel. A brilliant artist, he had designed murals in the dining room and the artwork on the menus. He was up early and went to bed late. When there were problems in the middle of the night, it was he who tended to the guests. The family paid him a meager salary and even deducted the costs of his art supplies. His monthly pay was so little he could not afford to buy a pair of pants. When a local church was asked to look into his welfare, the boy simply disappeared. Officials refused to pursue the matter.

impacts on ecology

Tourism development, even in "ecotourism" destinations, is often at odds with both ecological preservation and local use. The large numbers of tourists going to these places greatly exceed the carrying capacities—the amount of people a land can accommodate without ecological degradation. Most tourism destinations are energy intensive and highly pollutive and tend to be built in "cluster sites," such as a chain of hotels along a beach. This pattern of development diverts resources (energy, land, and water) away from the local population to accommodate the tourist sector. It also puts heavy stress on the environment, since tourist sites require

DEBORAH MCLAREN, ECUADOR

Hermes, a child laborer in the tourism industry in Ecuador, is missing after tourists inquired about his welfare.

reconstruction of the landscape and increased use of petroleum products and toxics such as chemicals, fertilizers, and pesticides. These cluster sites greatly disturb natural human patterns of living and are at odds with wildlife and the natural world.

The ecological damage done by tourism leads to battles between locals and the tourism industry for dwindling natural resources. A tourism researcher in Thailand explains how villagers must compete with tourists for the use of water in Phuket, Thailand:

> A single local village only needs one half cubic meter of fresh water per day. This amount is not enough for one guest staying in a hotel. More fresh water is needed for showers, toilets, baths, swimming pools and golf courses, as well. The fresh water use for ten big hotels in Phuket—about 100,000 cubic meters per day—equals the water used by the whole local Phuket population. In the dry season, when the underground water supplies dry up, many big hotels have to buy fresh water from the mainland, leaving the locals to find their own.[31]

The most popular trekking routes in Nepal attract more than 60,000 visitors a year to the Annapurna Mountains. The ensuing demand for fuel, especially local firewood, has had enormous consequences. Each of the

60,000 visitors spends a minimum of seven nights in the area—a total of 420,000 person/nights where fuel is needed for cooking, showers, and heat. According to Nepali government figures, a single trekker uses twice the amount of wood a local household member would require. This demand is obviously much more than the local area can provide. With the threat to survival so great, can host destinations afford tourism? Can the benefits that they gain economically offset the other demands—in this case, depletion of the natural resources that a community must endure at the hands of mass tourism development?

Some politicians have turned their attention to environmental issues, and tourism is proposed as a way to gain economic benefits and protect the environment. Costa Rica has an extensive system of national parks and reserves designed to protect the many ecosystems that attract tourists. It is doubtful that this model of ecotourism really works. "The politicians talk a lot about a new ecological order, but they don't do anything concrete," says Guillermo Canessa, executive director of the Costa Rican Association for the Conservation of Nature (ASCONA). "The country gets an award from the American Association of Travel Agents, but meanwhile we're watching our forests disappear, and the reforestation incentives are mostly benefiting big businesses."[32] In fact the parks lack sufficient funding to upgrade visitor facilities or manage the land in the face of increasing pressure from loggers, hunters, colonists, and spiraling numbers of tourists. And neither the foreign tourists who are flocking to the nation's protected areas nor the tour companies that bring them there are contributing to their maintenance.

new community realities

An example of one town that decided the costs of tourism were too great is Hanalei, a small community on the island of Kauai, Hawaii, where residents are at odds with hordes of tourists. Local boat owners began taking tourists around their coastline to view the fabulous natural sea caves and waterfalls. But according to tourism activist James Stark,

> The tour boat business has become an environmental nightmare. . . .
> Just over ten years ago, a local resident purchased a boat and began
> taking a handful of tourists on trips down the Na Pali Coast. . . .
> Other family-run operations started up. Initially, the small business
> integrated well into the community, providing a reasonable income
> for some residents of Hanalei and . . . not interfer[ing] with the

quality of life within the community. However, soon outside entrepreneurs realizing the financial potential of the rafting tours in the area began to set up operations in Hanalei. Now, the small community's main street is lined with 27 tour boats . . . carrying up to 1,400 tourists seven days a week.[33]

Business relationships between locals and outsiders have soured in Hanalei. The tour boats have taken over traditionally public space, which local Hawaiian families can no longer use. The new tour guides are not from the area and cannot provide tourists with accurate information. The influx of gas- and oil-powered boats has increased the environmental damage to the fragile coastline and sea caves in the area. Stark relates, "In the past, the businesses employed local residents, but now the majority of the jobs is taken by newcomers to Hanalei and most of the companies are owned by outsiders. The tour operators claim that their businesses are necessary in order to attract tourists outside of Hanalei. However, the people of the community feel that the tourists are actually attracted by the quality of life in Hanalei, rather than the adventure tours."[34]

Once outsiders become "insiders" and part of the community, the original inhabitants lose control over their lives. Businesses owned by outsiders have enormous political influence on policies and decisionmaking. Since the purpose of companies is to increase tourism and profits, their goal is to garner bigger shares of the tourist market. It is a never-ending cycle. Those fighting globalization believe citizens of the global South and North must form "chains," alliances built from experience. Solid support for regional trade and local self-reliance are crucial to the success of this effort. Small, local, responsible businesses need support in their battles against large corporations that consume enormous amounts of resources. These reforms would help to stem the tide of migration, lessen competition, and reduce environmental destruction.

Locals and tourists must recognize the great potential for utilizing the tourism industry as a tool for organizing, for establishing links between diverse sectors of people who are interested in being more than just tourists or just welcoming, smiling locals. This is not simply to encourage alternative tourism but actively to work against an exploitative global industry. As responsible tourism networks increase, there are opportunities for locals to gain outside support and information that can help them in their own communities and create international pressure. These networks are established and operated by people and organizations who are rethinking tourism, promoting responsibility, and linking with like-minded locals and tourists.

Some residents recently became fed up with irresponsible cruise ships at their Caribbean port that filled the area with snorkelers who were damaging the reefs and threatening the local fishing economy, trashing the city, and leaving at sunset. The cruise passengers didn't even eat in the town; the cruise ship was a mobile resort that simply floated away without any sense of obligation to the community. A request for support was sent out over the Internet. "Help!" the message said, "We have tried to talk to the cruise ship managers but they won't meet with us. We need the names of the top people at the company headquarters in Miami." Quickly responses came in: "I'll get that information and put pressure on them here," said one from the United States. Another suggestion was to organize international pressure on the company's stockholders. Within a few minutes, word of their plight had spread not only through North America and the Caribbean but to Europe and Asia. Consumer activists, environmentalists, and multinational watchdogs were informed. NGOs throughout the region, concerned tourists, students, and researchers who read alternative tourism bulletin boards were alerted. More suggestions poured in. International antitourism strategies were formed virtually overnight. Depending on the response from the cruise lines, an international campaign may form, which could certainly be of interest to the media. While this incident will not solve overall problems with the cruise lines or with tourism in that particular community, it is an example of people-to-people organizing and may encourage individuals to undertake a wider analysis of the problems with tourism.

notes

1. Helena Norberg-Hodge, *Ancient Futures: Learning from Ladakh* (San Francisco: Sierra Club Books, 1991), pp. 94–95. The pressure to modernize, argues Norberg-Hodge, stems from the psychological pressure that consumerism and conventional development has focused on unprepared cultures. The luxurious images of consumerism are enforced through media and tourism and create artificial "needs" previously unknown in self-sufficient traditional cultures. These "needs" contribute to insecurity and loss of self-esteem and create an artificial scarcity that puts people who were traditionally close-knit in competition with each other and pressures them to conform to Western models they cannot emulate. Norberg-Hodge presents this concept more fully in the essay "The Pressure to Modernize," in Edward Goldsmith, Martin Khor, Helena Norberg-Hodge, and Vandana Shiva, *The Future of Progress: Reflections on Environment and Development* (Berkeley: International Society for Ecology and Culture, 1992), pp. 81–100.
2. Quoted from "The Facts," a compilation of tourist arrivals from the World Tourism Organization, *New Internationalist* 245 (1993), p. 19.

3. "The Facts," p. 19.
4. "The Facts," p. 13.
5. M. Kelly, "West Beach Is Only the Beginning for Wai'Anae," *Contours* (Bangkok) 3(7): 17.
6. Kelly, "West Beach" p. 17.
7. Jean Keefe, "Whose Home Is It Anyway?" *In Focus*, Spring 1995, p. 5.
8. Keefe, "Whose Home," p. 5.
9. Chee Yoke Ling, "A Rough Deal: Golf Displaces People," *In Focus*, Spring 1995, p. 12.
10. Ling, "A Rough Deal," p. 13.
11. Ling, "A Rough Deal," p. 13.
12. Quoted from *Responsible Cruising: Background Information*. Brochure available from the Center for Seafarers Rights, New York, and the Center for Responsible Tourism, San Anselmo, CA.
13. *Responsible Cruising*.
14. Valene L. Smith, ed., *Hosts and Guests: The Anthropology of Tourism*, 2nd ed. (Philadelphia: University of Pennsylvania Press, 1989), p. 8.
15. Norberg-Hodge, *Ancient Futures*, p. 109.
16. Norberg-Hodge, "The Pressure to Modernize," p. 81.
17. Wiert Wiertsema, "Paths to Sustainability," in Edward Goldsmith, Martin Khor, Helena Norberg-Hodge, and Vandana Shiva, *The Future of Progress: Reflections on Environment and Development* (Berkeley: International Society for Ecology and Culture, 1992), p. 167.
18. Matthew Rothschild, "Multinational Corporations: Affecting Lives on a Global Scale," in *Native Resource Control and the Multinational Corporate Challenge: Aboriginal Rights in International Perspective* (Cambridge: Cultural Survival, Anthropology Resource Center, 1982), p. 8.
19. Linda K. Richter, "Indonesian Tourism: The Good, the Bad and the Ugly," *Contours* (ECTWT: Bangkok) 14(1): 29–30.
20. Yareth Rosen, "Last Frontier Image Pulls Growing Crowd of Tourists to Alaska," *Christian Science Monitor*, August 19, 1991, p. 9.
21. Vine Deloria Jr. and Clifford M. Lytle, *American Indians, American Justice* (Austin: University of Texas Press, 1983), p. 7.
22. Kaleo Patterson, "Aloha! Welcome to Paradise," *New Internationalist* 245 (1993), p. 15.
23. Ritchie Witzig, "New and Old Disease Threats in the Peruvian Amazon: The Case of the Urarina," *Abya Yala News: Journal of the South and Meso American Indian Rights Center*, Summer 1996, pp. 6–7.
24. Witzig, "New and Old," pp. 7, 9.
25. Witzig, "New and Old," p. 7.
26. Witzig, "New and Old," p. 7.
27. Witzig, "New and Old," p. 46.
28. Quoted from "Boy Prostitution in Sri Lanka," *Prostitution Tourism Development Documentation* (report includes news clips and other information and is available from ECTWT, Bangkok, n.d.), 31.
29. Sue Wheat, "Tourism: An Unwanted Guest?" *Tibet News* (London) 20 (1996): 5.

30. D. H. Donnelly, *Where Have All the Children Gone?* reported in an alert from Broken Bud, Berkeley, CA, 1996, p. 1.
31. Kund Daeng, "Alternative Tourism," *Alternative Tour Thailand* 2 (1990): 3.
32. David Dudenhoefer, "Ecotourism Boom Forces Nation to Seek New Alternatives," 1991–1992 *Guide to Costa Rica* (San Jose: *Tico Times*, 1991), p. 9.
33. James Stark, "Hawaii: Tourism Action Network," *Contours* (ECTWT: Bangkok) 4(4): 20.
34. Stark, "Hawaii," 20.

5

rethinking ecotravel

$e$cotravel involves activities in the great outdoors—nature tourism, adventure travel, birding, camping, skiing, whale watching, and archaeological digs that take place in marine, mountain, island, and desert ecosystems. Much of this travel is now called ecotourism, although critics argue that the definition of "eco-tourism" is so broad that almost any travel would qualify, as long as something green was seen along the way. John Shores, who has written about ecotourism, says its "goal posts are spread so far that every attempt scores a goal. This adversely affects protected areas and biodiversity in several ways. . . . Continued use of all-encompassing definitions in the nature-tourism arena weakens the power of the concept, contributes to ambiguity, and encourages misuse and abuse of the idea."[1]

I use the term "ecotravel" to encompass all forms of ecotourism, conservation-focused tourism, and other types of nature travel that market the earth. The popular term, "ecotourism," is not limited to visits to natural areas. The number of tourists who travel solely to view natural surroundings or wildlife is actually quite modest. A majority of travelers also want an opportunity to experience a culture different from their own. Cultural activities and lifestyles are featured prominently in travel brochures. Ecotravel programs cover a wide variety of experiences—from spartan, hard-core, bury-your-own-poop backpacking in special conservation zones to the purely hedonistic, luxury vacations at typical resorts. They offer a participatory experience in the natural environment. At its best ecotravel promotes environmental conservation, international understanding and cooperation, political and economic empowerment of local populations, and cultural preservation. When ecotravel fulfills its mission, it not only has a minimal impact, but the local environment and community actually benefit from the experience and even own or control it. At its worst ecotravel is environmentally destructive, economically exploitative, culturally insensitive, "greenwashed" travel.

Most ecotravel is simply a way to get out of urban environments and back to nature, or to the nature that existed before human systems came to dominate it. But whatever the motive, the effects of global tourism on the environment are potentially terrifying. Huge amounts of fossil fuel are required for all forms of transportation. Tourists create a transient but permanent population increase in destination sites. The land required for expanding tourist sites around the world disturbs the ecological balance. Finally, tourism creates monumental waste and pollution. The result of all these secondary effects of tourism working in tandem is a rapidly shrinking land mass.

Ecotourism developed from different motives: conserving the environment, providing nature-based and adventure travel, and serving the growing tourist demand for more "authentic" experiences. While ecotourism has brought attention to the conservation of pristine areas, the reality is that tourism is not ecofriendly. An ecotourist, like any tourist, uses tremendous amounts of natural resources to jet halfway around the world to enjoy an outdoor experience. According to the World Watch Institute, "Airplanes are the most energy-intensive means of carrying people and cargo."[2] World Watch reports that jet travel's impact on climate warming is a growing concern, as "commercial aircraft may be a major catalyst of the greenhouse effect due to the peculiarities of high-altitude flight."[3] Scientists calculate that each year airplanes produce nearly four million tons of nitrogen oxides, which react with sunlight to form ozone, a potent heat trapper; "nitrogen oxides from aircraft could be responsible for more than 30 percent of future global warming."[4]

Ecotourism's popularity is actually magnifying the negative impacts upon the earth, since it promotes development (destruction) of wilderness. For a tourist to have truly minimal impact, she would have to walk to the destination, use no natural resources, and bring her own food that she grew and harvested. She would also have to carry along her own low-impact accommodations (a tent) or stay in a place that is locally owned and uses alternative technologies and waste treatment. Of course she would also leave the destination in no worse and perhaps in even better condition than she found it and contribute funds to local environmental protection and community development.

But conservationists and government planners cite many reasons why ecotravel to protected areas can be advantageous. They believe ecotravel is a subjectively healthier kind of tourism that attracts desirable visitors. Since ecotravelers are often more tolerant of rustic, basic facilities and infrastructure, tourism inflow can be increased without major expenditures. In some cases ecotourism can support the capital improvements over the long term, starting with just a trickle of undemanding tourists who prefer small-scale accommodations built by local people with native rather than costly and pretentious tourist facilities. Protection of certain natural areas for tourism encourages land use planning. In theory, rural communities will receive the economic benefits of ecotourism. Ideally, ecotourism's profits will help local people; they will in turn participate in integrated, regional planning. Ecotourism may actually be worse for Indigenous Peoples and other rural communities since they have fewer facilities to support increased tourist populations and fewer policies and regulations to monitor its development than do other tourist destinations.

The tourism industry regards ecotourism as an exciting new product to market; environmental groups tend to see it more as a means of conservation and protection. A number of environmental groups and socially responsible organizations have joined the ecotourism industry, looking for ways to promote and finance conservation efforts and developed the first models of ecotourism by using tourist fees to support conservation work. Initially, the targets of conservation were wildlife areas and national parks. International laws were implemented to protect endangered species, and large parcels of land were set aside as protected areas.

Many of these conservation projects were opposed by local people and created conflicts in the nearby communities. And because of the fragility of the favored areas, the increased numbers of tourists soon began to take a toll on the environment. The original designers of ecotourism realized that ecotourists were loving nature to death and disrupting the lives of local people. Despite such problems, many countries have sought new ways to address development issues by incorporating tourism. The World Wildlife Fund reported that

> countries or regions lacking in other natural resources came to regard a favorable climate, beaches, and other tourist attractions as a different type of natural resource base for development. Since many of these countries had already established parks and protected areas, promoting tourism seemed an easy way for them to benefit. According to the International Union for the Conservation of Nature and Natural Resources (IUCN), national parks in the tropics—approximately 1,420 individual areas covering over 175 million hectares—now play an important role in promoting tourism in almost all tropical countries.[5]

The American Society of Travel Agents reported that in contrast to the 1980s (the decade of overt materialism and consumption), American consumers are predicted to become more socially conscious and embrace simpler lifestyles in the 1990s.[6] Sophisticated marketers, advertisers, and travel agents will cater to a more demanding consumer by improving and supporting ecotourism programs and other nature-based, culturally sensitive travel.

ecotourism saves the planet?

Academic study programs with an environmental twist have boomed. University Research Expeditions, the School for International Field Studies, Earthwatch Expeditions, the Sierra Club travel programs, and other programs deliver thousands of new-breed ecostudents to tag turtles, bag leeches, and count plants in the wilds. And yet there has been little analysis of the long-term impacts of ecotourism. The few reports that exist suggest that projects have failed to achieve the promised conservation or economic benefits. No one knows how the environment will be affected by millions of people traveling around the world, using resources and invading fragile areas. Paul Erlich warns, "We are not able to support the present population on income from our natural capital: we're only doing it by exhausting our capital. That's a one-way street."[7]

Each community and culture has a different response to tourism. While some are working cooperatively with private enterprise, others feel they are being invaded by tourists, just as they are by other colonists who take over their homelands. In Chiapas, Mexico, there has been organized resistance to massive tourism plans for the Mayan Biosphere, and in Nagarhole, India, Indigenous People living in a national park were supported by an international campaign to resist tourism construction and their displacement from traditional lands by an "ecoresort." Most Indigenous lands have been turned into federal parks, refuges, cultural heritage sites, and monuments. These designations conflict with local use or multiple use traditions.

Since the 1970s the concept of conservation has emerged as a mandate that land should be preserved in its natural state. Such a mandate can infringe on traditional lifestyles by limiting subsistence activities. It is difficult to comprehend the myriad of complex issues Indigenous Peoples face, often without the proper knowledge and tools to plan for their futures. Many Indigenous communities hope that ecotourism will be a way to resist other destructive forms of development. They are alert to ecotourism strategies to protect their natural resources, environments, and cultures. But some have seen such projects backfire, creating conflicts and divisions within their communities. There are no easy answers, but it is essential that information be shared with Indigenous communities confronting tourism development.

national players and effects on community economics

Ecotravel is big business. It has greatly expanded jobs for tourism corporations, adventure travel companies, environmental organizations, and government officials. However, the scope of the ecotourism market is hard to gauge since there is little agreement regarding the definition of ecotourism. It is further complicated by the incomplete record-keeping of most host countries.

Ecotourism projects run the gamut from small-scale to monstrous. While many ecotour operators limit group size to ten or twelve people, ecoresorts are being designed to accommodate thousands of people at once. In terms of land area, there are small ecotourism projects that encompass just a few acres and others that encompass hundreds or thousands of square miles. The La Ruta Maya and La Selva projects cover parts of five countries in Central America.

Just how the income from ecotourism fees is distributed is difficult to determine. A major portion of the money generated on-site goes to maintaining the tourist attraction and hotels, staff, infrastructure, technical assistance, training, and other things contracted by the public sector. Once the private-sector costs are deducted, any remaining funds could be used to address issues such as encroachment around the ecotourism site. There are no examples of ecotourism projects that adequately pay for themselves; in other words, ecotourism is simply not sustainable.

New forms of ecotravel are supposed to save the planet and create economic advantages for local people. In reality few of ecotourism's benefits go to locals. "A study of twenty-three protected areas with projects designed to generate local economic development found that while many projects promoted ecotourism, few generated substantial benefits for either parks or local people."[8] More integrated approaches designed to generate local economic development have created relatively few jobs. Even at highly successful parks, such as KhaoYai National Park in Thailand, where tourists bring in about $5 million annually, the surrounding communities remain poor. Ecotourism revenues in Rwanda

More than 60,000 annual trekkers along with the porters and pack animals they require have caused serious erosion in the Annapurna Circuit in Nepal; some ruts are several feet deep.

DEBORAH MCLAREN, NEPAL

support the park system and the central government, but few economic alternatives exist for local populations.9

For any real benefits from ecotourism, local people must be involved in every stage, from the initial planning through the development, monitoring, enforcement, and ownership. In Costa Rica, considered a model ecotourism destination, many biological reserves and stands of old-growth forest are owned by foreigners. One local commmnity has formed an association to buy back these lands. "With the development of the ecotourism industry, local residents have garnered some benefits as employees of ecotourism entrepreneurs, but there seems to be no example of a local resident who is owner of a successful ecotourism establishment."10 The locals hope some day to develop their own ecotourism operations.

environmental effects

The issues involved in ecotravel epitomize what is happening with tourism around the world. If ecotravel creates enormous environmental devastation when it is supposed to be "good" for the environment, what are the effects of conventional tourism on the environment? If ecotravel is the best-case scenario, what is the worst? There are numerous examples of worst-case scenarios just in the United States. The beloved Grand Canyon is not designated as an ecotourism destination, but it is the forerunner of all such ecotravel programs and an excellent object of study regarding long-term impacts. Despite the number of tourists and the money spent to keep it up, the federal government can no longer manage it. According to Julie Galton Gale of the Grand Canyon Trust,

> There are simply too many people, too many cars, too many airplanes. Despite current laws restricting flights, there were over 800,000 tour flights over the Grand Canyon in 1996. The Grand Canyon would be completely overrun if Park Service allowed tour operators free rein. Another problem is the incursion of roads and trails . . . in areas that were previously inaccessible. The impacts on local communities is dramatic. This is a place that got "discovered" because of the increase in tourism development. Now they're building a Wal-Mart in Moab. There are no zoning laws; it's one hotel after fast food restaurant. The detrimental growth is directly a result of having been discovered as an "outdoor adventure" destination.[11]

The Grand Canyon Trust works with communities on the Colorado Plateau affected by tourism. They say there is an urgent need for education of local citizens, elected officials, and tourists and more integrated planning, dispute resolution, better forms of energy, and alternatives to harvesting old-growth timber. If we cannot stop the environmental destruction of the Grand Canyon, there is little hope for the national parks that Western conservationists are planning in other parts of the world.

ecotourism's new international players

New concepts in tourism that focus on sustainable development and ecotourism have opened the door for further expansion of the global industry. National government agencies, development agencies, private enterprise, and the World Bank are becoming infatuated with ecotourism programs. Northern environmental NGOs are providing abundant financing for ecotourism. New ideas for tourism have consistently proven problematic since they follow the traditional path of development and are often initiated in the global North. Attempts to link ecotourism to other sustainable development projects have been controversial, especially when tied to development strategies such as economic initiatives to market sustainable use products from the rain forests, collect medicinal plants, or cement other bioprospecting agreements with universities and pharmaceutical companies.

Tourism has long been of interest to U.S. government agencies. USAID recently renewed its interest in ecotourism. Its goal is to promote environmentally sound, long-term economic growth, often developing natural areas for their "sustainable yield." USAID has placed high priority on stimulating private investment, free markets, and free enterprise and regards "nature-based tourism as well suited for simultaneously meeting" these objectives.[12] The Latin America and Caribbean Bureau of USAID operate ecotourism projects, mainly in national parks; the Africa Bureau "recently investigated the possibility of sport hunting in the northwestern Karamoja region of Uganda."[13]

The National Oceanic and Atmospheric Agency's National Marine Fisheries Services provides technical assistance for tourism development related to saltwater sport fishing. The Overseas Private Investment Corporation (OPIC) funds ecotourism-related projects and "has the potential to become a major source of financing for the ecotourism industry through its new 'Environmental Investment Fund' . . . which funds ecotourism projects such as guest lodges near natural attractions."[14]

Multilateral financial institutions support ecotourism because it stimulates economic development. Yet many environmental groups, Indigenous Peoples, and other local people say the government and multilateral institutions neglect to include them in their programs. The World Bank, for example, does not have a good history when it comes to tourism. In 1969 the World Bank created a tourism department that lent over $450 million directly to twenty-four tourism projects in eighteen countries throughout the developing world. The department was discontinued because of the "bad publicity associated with funding capital intensive projects, such as large hotels, which clashed with the Bank's evolving rural poor mandate."[15]

Currently the World Bank has no real policy for tourism development; although its policies for working with Indigenous Peoples, protecting the environment, and encouraging participation of affected people should apply, they are often ignored. The Global Environment Facility (GEF), an arm of the World Bank, is currently undertaking ecotourism development under the term "biodiversity protection" in several countries. Some of the projects have been opposed by environmentalists and Indigenous organizations. However, the GEF bypasses these locals and links with more "cooperative" groups to continue the projects.

Many governments are becoming international players as they claim to be developing ecotourism projects, yet these programs are coming at a great expense to the environment. One of the worst acts of "ecoterrorism" yet, according to a watch group in Thailand, is "unbelievable! In the name of ecotourism the Lao government has given the green light to the Malaysian Syuen Corporation to develop a mammoth resort [in a] national park. . . . to pave the way for the US $211 million 'Phou Khao Khouay-Nam Ngum Ecotourism Resort,' including a minicity of hotels, golf courses, casinos. . . . Local residents have to move out of the area."[16]

examples of eco-oh-ohs!

From overpopulation that threatens both wildlife and people in the Galapagos, to "green" corporations, to land development paving the way for ecotravel, the problems are growing rapidly. Lands have been cleared and locals displaced for a huge dam project to provide ecotravelers with electricity in Malaysia. Elsewhere around the world developers are building major airports to bring in more ecotravelers and the imports they require to set up golf courses, ecoresorts, ecocondominiums, ecolodges, ecomarine parks, and ecoranches. There is a limit to how far tourism can go toward rescuing an economy, however.

selling out in costa rica. In Costa Rica the ecodevelopment Papagayo Project is the center of controversy. The massive project includes the construction of 1,144 homes, 6,270 condo-hotel units, 6,584 hotel rooms, a shopping center, and a golf course along the shores of Bahia Culebra.

> The enormous scope of this project is entirely inconsistent with the concept of sustainable and socially responsible ecotourism. . . . The use of the title "Ecodesarrollo Papagayo" [Ecodevelopment Papagayo] is a sad attempt to disguise this huge construction project under the all-too abused umbrella of ecotourism. The project has nothing to do with ecology, much less with responsible development for Costa Rica. Papagayo is nothing more than a high-profit real estate scheme designed to make a bundle of money for a few Costa Rican investors and their foreign corporate allies.[17]

Costa Rica has lost sight of small, locally owned accommodations and conservation and is moving toward privatization and the development of megaresorts. Costa Rica guidebooks are full of advertisements inviting tourists to pick out the piece of virgin forest or beach they would like to purchase, many promising, "American construction company on-site." Tours have turned into real estate outings for foreigners. Since Costa Rica is considered the ecotourism model of the world, we should take note of how this "perfect" example of ecotravel exploits nature, conservation ideas, and locals by selling lands, constructing megaresorts, and otherwise paving paradise. It has become the ultimate ecotourism lie.

the galapagos islands: tourist evolution crowding out other species. The Galapagos Islands, long considered a model for tourism management worldwide, today face new perils from tourists and from the booming immigration of Ecuadorans from the mainland looking for jobs. Fascination with the islands' fabled flora and fauna may lead to their demise. The Galapagos are at an evolutionary crossroad. Nearly 60,000 visitors toured the islands in 1994, despite the government's limit of 25,000 (in effect since 1982). A rise in the number of boat licenses and proposed construction of luxury hotels in the islands magnify the threats.

Christophe Grenier spent a year and a half researching tourism impacts and conservation in the Galapagos and conducted a survey of almost 2,000 tourists and locals. Grenier says the ecological damage is "being done at a terrific speed: more people, tourists, boats, cars, concrete, introduced plants and animals, and the boom for sharks for Asian markets." The Ecuadoran government is incapable of stopping this disastrous evolution:

> The government, the Darwin Foundation, and some international experts developed tourism policy for the Galapagos and want to limit migration by reducing the monetary flow poured by tourism into the local economy. This policy is actually "selective tourism" although it claims to be ecotourism. The goal is to transform the islands into an expensive tour destination—higher airline prices, higher national park taxes, higher yacht tariffs—so it will discourage the "cheap" tourists, who contribute directly to the locals. The result is both tourists and prices have increased while limits are not enforced. The Galapagos National Park Service allows cruise boats while it's officially forbidden. Migration continues and the lack of local jobs in the tourist economy has resulted in people taking jobs in illegal fisheries, which have boomed. The ecological degradation is very rapid while the locals oppose any type of conservation. The locals believe the Foundation naturalists don't care about human beings living in the archipelago, partly because they use the islands' nature to make money. Thirty to forty percent of the Darwin Foundation budget comes from tourist donations. What I have learned about conservation is that there is no way to protect

natural areas without putting their inhabitants at the core of conservation policy.[18]

malaysia's ecomisadventure. In Bakun, Sarawak, the
building of a 2,400-megawatt hydroelectric dam to cater to Malaysia's
power needs is now connected to the development of tourism. According
to Sue Wheat, "The dam will involve flooding and clearing 70,000
hectares of land—roughly equivalent to the size of Singapore—and the
8,000 people who will be displaced are protesting against the development, insisting they have Native Customary Rights to the land."[19] Wheat
spoke to representatives of the Sarawak Solidarity Campaign, which
opposes the development. The campaign argues that the government,
timber industry, construction companies, and tourism all have stakes in
one another's businesses and are unified in support of the dam project.
Wheat believes it is in the corporations' interests to continue the development of the dam under the banner of ecotourism.

the himalayan ecotourism experience. Recent reports
about the Annapurna Conservation Area Project (ACAP) in Nepal, one
of the oldest ecotravel programs, indicate it has not provided the benefits
initially anticipated. According to evaluations undertaken by the World
Wildlife Fund,[20] it has spawned only menial jobs for porters who carry
tourists' supplies and gear up and down the world's steepest mountains.
Beyond the forty or fifty families that live directly along the trekking
routes, there has been minimal trickle-down economic benefit. ACAP
has little interaction with the tourism industry in Nepal. While income
generated by trekkers fees goes mainly to the military for park protection,
the fees have also helped offset some of the impacts created by tourism;
trail maintenance projects, poultry farming, and sanitation programs have
been implemented.

the (golf) "greens" conquer paradise. As in the case of
Costa Rica, many new ecoprojects now include golf courses, though few
environmentalists would promote golf courses as a sustainable tourism
option, since they put pollution, herbicides, pesticides, and contaminated
water into the natural environment; take up huge amounts of land that
is often needed for agriculture; and displace farmers and traditional communities. But in the 1990s hundreds of golf courses were built throughout Asia and the Pacific. At the United Nations–sponsored World Food
Summit in 1996, it was pointed out that golf had in effect taken

food out of people's mouths. . . . If tens of thousands of hectares
wasted on golf course construction had been planted in grain, it
would have supported hundreds of thousands of people. . . .

DEBORAH MCLAREN, NORTHERN THAILAND

With no recycling or waste management, plastic trash (brought in by tourists) accumulates behind trekker huts in Thailand. Local people must burn the plastic, causing hazardous toxic chemicals to be released.

> Building golf courses has led to the destruction of forests and farmland and also drained much-needed water from agricultural use in the area. . . . [One expert said,] "Tourist earnings may be important but golf courses are catering to an upper elite and contribute little to the welfare of the 1.2 billion people in the world believed to be surviving on less than US$1 a day."[21]

"greening" and "sustaining" the tourism industry

Ecotourism is supposed to mean ecologically sound tourism. It implies that one would take care of a place just as one would take care of one's own home. Yet how many ecotravelers are actively involved in environmental preservation in their own communities? It is important for all travelers to link their travels to their work and interests in their own communities. When we understand what is at stake, we can join with other people around the world and better confront the environmental challenges we face together.

Ecoterminology and philosophy continue to mutate. Just when we thought we might understand "ecotourism," environmentalists and futurists warn that we must develop "sustainable" patterns of tourism development. "Sustainable tourism development" has been defined as meeting the needs of present tourists and host regions while protecting and enhancing opportunities for the future. Sustainability is a concept that is not easy to translate into specific actions that individuals or governments can undertake. Critics suggest that sustainability is based on Western values and economic models developed on an anti-ecological basis, and early visions for sustainability fail to challenge some of the basic premises that have helped us into the environmental mess we are now in. Others warn that the term has become co-opted by private industry and is a "green" stamp of approval for business as usual—a trend that we will see more of in the future. One thing is certain: "sustainability" as a concept is used to promote the World Bank's reentrance into tourism and as a basis for many environmental organizations' work in the global South.

Many countries are promoting so-called sustainable development schemes that are nothing more than conventional tourism. These schemes camouflage themselves under green banners while building massive infrastructures and inviting unbridled numbers of tourists into fragile environments, historical places, and Indigenous homelands. Some of these strategies are under fire from locals who say the projects have huge budgets to promote their greenwashing of tourism and in reality are doing little to accomplish the sustainable strategies they claim they are developing. A recent statement from the Tourism Authority of Thailand (TAT) reflects the sustainability push: "The TAT is committed to developing tourism in a way that is environmentally responsible, and in harmony with the needs of local communities." But according to a Thai tourism watch group, Towards Ecological Recovery and Regional Alliance (TERRA), "TAT's priority has always been to promote and market tourism, and it is a well established fact that it has little, if any, experience with environmental protection and community development. Currently, more than US$40 million of TAT's fiscal budget is allocated to domestic and international marketing schemes, while only US$12 million is set aside for tourism resource development."[22]

In addition, many ecotourism programs are designed using commercialized conservation methods. This means that the value of natural resources and conservation efforts are measured purely in economic terms, according to present or future profitability, without taking into account the inherent ecological value of the environment. This formula simply sets aside land as "reserved" and does not address root causes of development expansion and colonization.

Truly sustainable tourism must be locally controlled, limited, and focus on local self-reliance without diminishing local resources for the local population. Sustainable tourism would include integrated planning that challenges the tourism industry at every level. It would take up broad issues, from the reduction of energy-consumptive technologies to the society's religious practices, and would most likely be an impetus to halt further tourism development.

strategies for rethinking ecotravel

Since all forms of tourism are unsustainable and Western development processes are threatening both biological and cultural diversity in every destination community around the world, true efforts toward ecotourism would move away from specific conservation and environmental protection strategies to integrate broad community and regional development priorities. Primary components would focus on education and promote critical thinking about development, growth-oriented economics, and other unsustainable practices; the strategies would design programs to counter the ideologies and effects of unsustainable, consumptive models of development. These projects would not only develop alternative tourism but would rethink these strategies as well.

In Ladakh, India, the community has created the Ladakh Ecological and Development Group (LedeG), which teaches tourists and locals about the impacts of tourism on their culture and environment. From their solar-powered ecology center in the capital, Leh, they have helped introduce appropriate technologies, organized cultural programs to pass down knowledge and skills from elders to young people, and recruited tourists to volunteer labor for many of their projects. Many community projects—including the establishment of youth groups and women's groups—have resulted from their work. Because of the LedeG, both young and old people are involved in a critical analysis of the Western processes that are now invading their cultures.

In other places around the world, people are beginning to work actively against tourism development in their communities. Many resourceful activists are intent upon taking tourism a step further. The responsible tourism movement has emerged from a number of concerns. It is designed primarily to make people-to-people connections so that citizens of the world can experience the realities of other societies and environments. This type of tourism is based on the principle that people matter and that humans are basically dependent upon—and responsible for—the earth's resources. Connecting with each other at a human level allows both the so-called hosts and guests to observe and learn from one another in more equitable, realistic terms. Most strategies for actively negating traditional, exploitative tourism practices are on a small scale. From tour operators to regional strategies developing from local communities, this is where some of the best new ideas emerge. Himalayan High Treks is an example of a small business that works to offset the effects of tourism. Owner Effie Fletcher told me,

> I'm concerned about locals' maintaining their traditional lifestyle. Development, unjust economics and Westernization have made many so poor they must sell their animals, pack up, and move to a job in the city. They don't have the option to stay and have a pristine lifestyle: the land is gone, split up, and subdivided. Many tourists want to be "the first" and seek out pristine environments. I have strong opinions about that—there is no need to continue to simply exploit new territories when, as tourists, we have some responsibility for the problems we've helped to create. We [at Himalayan High Treks] go to impacted areas and work with locals to lessen those impacts. We use locally owned and produced items and services, eat local food, stay at local guest houses. It's much more expensive to do the research. It would be easier to fax and phone big hotels. But it's our responsibility and an investment in the future.

Where are the most successful ecotravel programs and policies formed? Invariably, they come from grassroots organizations that link with responsible tourism groups to develop educational programs. These ideas integrate real change and take the focus off of marketing "green" tourism or zoning off wilderness areas. Luciano Minerbi, a professor at the University of Hawaii at Manoa and a member of the Hawaii Ecumenical Coalition on Tourism, has worked with Native Hawaiians to develop eco-cultural tourism. According to Minerbi, their goals include:

- allowing Indigenous Peoples back on their lands and promoting experimental homesteading arrangements, subsistence economies, and affordable and appropriate modern and Indigenous technologies;
- promoting research and development of eco-industry involving local people with universities and industries;
- decentralizing environmental agencies so locals can develop and implement their own strategies;
- establishing partnerships among local communities,

schools, landowners, and the industry to provide opportunities to merge traditional knowledge with modern science;

- halting monocrop agriculture, which displaces locals and
leads to further development, deforestation, pollution, water
diversion, soil erosion, and destruction of sacred sites;
- halting speculation of real estate development for resorts,
golf courses, and the international market;
- allowing customary access to subsistence resources and religious sites and returning lands for community restoration;
- protecting and repossessing lands, particularly for community land trusts;
- undertaking cultural assessments to demarcate important
areas, map resources, and suggest protection programs;
- regulating but legalizing small, locally owned accommodations for community-based service organizations so economic benefits of visitors remain within the community;
- making Indigenous points of view known within the industry and to the public.[23]

In some communities local students and others are designing their own
"ecojustice tours" for locals to see firsthand the problems associated with
development in their communities and to meet with planners, scientists,
city officials, environmentalists, and community activists. Through these
tours many people have been inspired to work for protection of their communities and green spaces and to oppose environmental racism in areas
that are predominantly inhabited by people of color.

And whom do local people consider good tourists? The villagers of
Gundrung, Nepal, have on the wall of their community center a photograph of a smiling, bearded young man with a backpack. The villagers
say he was the best ecotourist ever to visit their community: he brought
much of his own food, stayed at a local's lodge, helped repair trails, and
was concerned about the villagers' use of fuel wood—he never asked to
take a hot shower. He even carried his own water jug to use in place of
toilet paper. They say they wish all ecotourists could be as sensitive and
helpful.

Some refute the growing crisis of the natural world and promote free
trade and unsustainable, high technologies to "solve" environmental problems. Even McDonald's is funding ecotourism projects now. McDonald's
Indonesia Family Restaurants is a partner with environmental organizations to develop local enterprises in and around Gunung Halimun
National Park, in West Java.[24] Perhaps the wave of the future is to have
McDonald's restaurants at all ecotourism destinations around the world.

Virtually every place on earth has experienced significant intrusion from humans. Even the Antarctic is littered with trash, toxic batteries, and plastics left by tour groups. Tourism is a population problem, for not only is the earth's population growing, but millions of people are not simply staying at home—they are consuming enormous amounts of natural resources to get to other places. These populations are transient but often mean a permanent population increase in destination communities. Yet the population problems associated with tourism are not taken seriously by population experts.

What is the difference between conventional travel and ecotravel? The overwhelming answer seems to be not much. Ecotravel may involve more of a focus on getting out to see nature, but that doesn't necessarily mean protecting the earth. Rethinking tourism means finding activities that might never be considered ecotravel by the travel industry but can contribute to real environmental protection of the earth. For example, human rights groups, labor unions, and environmental groups are linking with workers in sweatshops along the border of Mexico to conduct "reality" tours about the increasingly dismal state of the border area and gain support for broad issues. Environmental organizations, universities, and other research expeditions and study programs recruit tourists to undertake valuable field studies and restoration projects. Hikers are turning into advocates to preserve wilderness areas.

Sustainable agriculture has disappeared in places where tourism was but the first wave of an international corporate incursion. Tourism has displaced small farms and in some cases promoted unsustainable agriculture. In places where sustainable agriculture still exists, for example, Costa Rica and Mexico, monoculture agricultural processes have turned coffee exporting into a commercialized tourist venture. But new agricultural programs, eco-agro farms and villages, are concerned with self-sufficiency and local economies—promoting more control of investment, production, and sales; a healthier sense of community; and less reliance on the global economy. Eco-agro tourism is seen as a way to address problems in the agrarian sector. A recent study on this form of tourism in Poland reports, "One of the most interesting results concerns the fact that farmers and officials play into each other's hands. According to the officials the farmers should take the initiatives, according to the farmers the government and other institutions should provide financial and organizational support in order to make it possible to start agro-tourist activities."[25] Eco-agro tours offer tourists an opportunity to reconnect with the land—to learn about organic farming and less-consumptive technologies—and become committed to preserving it. Yet they work to have highly diversified local economies and refrain from relying on the tourism sector. These programs may be the most integrated approach to protection of the natural world: true ecotravel.

A group of organic farmers has created an eco-agro tourism network of more than 200 family farms worldwide and growing rapidly. More than 100 farms are part of the European Center for Eco-Agro Tourism (ECEAT), which promotes nature and lobbies politicians and the tourism sector to apply more integrated approaches in development policies and planning that relate to farming and agriculture. Members are involved in village restoration, conservation and waste management, and marketing organic foods. The farmers are organized in each country to support each other in a variety of ways, through linking, technical assistance, and policy. The eco-agro tourism initiative started by promoting organic farms, but the concept has widened to include programs with national parks, environmental NGOs, and sustainable villages and regions. Cooperena in Costa Rica is a cooperative consortium of small-scale, eco-agro tourism programs. Leila Solano, one of the program coordinators, told me, "This type of program spreads tourists through decentralized accommodations while supporting farmers and rural communities. . . . Eco-agro tourism is a step on the way toward a locally integrated plan that focuses on preserving the environment, agriculture and rural economies."

Rethinking tourism considers ecotravel and all other forms of alternative tourism as part of the massive global tourism industry. The effects of ecotravel are similar to conventional tourism and in many cases might even be worse, since it has encouraged a boom of tourists and development in regions that are fragile and remote, some of the most important biologically and culturally diverse areas on the planet. As Zac Goldsmith states, "The addition of the word 'eco' to the word 'tourism' has so far remained cosmetic. Tourism today is incompatible with life tomorrow. If as an industry it is to be made consistent with ecological and human principles, then we must examine it thoroughly, both the pros and cons, and must be prepared to re-think what may well be a fundamentally flawed process."[26] Ultimately, all tourism greatly costs the earth.

notes

1. John Shores, "Report on Ecotourism," available from 1828 Kilbourne Place, NW, Washington, DC 10010; e-mail Jshores@capaccess.org.
2. Hal Kane, "Air Travel Growth Resumes," *Vital Signs 1993: The Trends That Are Shaping Our Future* (New York: W. W. Norton and World Watch Institute, 1993), p. 90.

3. Kane, "Air Travel," p. 36.
4. Kane, "Air Travel," p. 36.
5. Elizabeth Boo, *Ecotourism: The Potentials and Pitfalls* (Washington, DC: World Wildlife Fund, 1989), p. 9.
6. U.S. Travel Data Center, *Tourism and the Environment* (Washington, DC: U.S. Travel Data Center and Travel Industry Association of America, 1992), p. 4.
7. Jim Motavalli, "Conversations: Paul and Anne Erlich," in *E: The Environmental Magazine*, November-December 1996, p. 10.
8. M. Wells and K. Brandon, *People and Parks: Linking Protected Area Management with Local Communities* (Washington, DC: World Bank, 1992), cited in Katrina Brandon, *Ecotourism and Conservation: A Review of Key Issues* (Washington, DC: World Bank, 1996), p. 11.
9. Brandon, *Ecotourism*, p. 11.
10. John Vandermeer and Ivette Perfecto, *Breakfast of Biodiversity: The Truth About Rain Forest Destruction* (Oakland: Food First and Institute for Food and Development Policy, 1995), p. 110.
11. Julie Galton Gale, interview with the author, January 1997.
12. USAID, *Ecotourism: A Viable Alternative for Sustainable Management of Natural Resources in Africa* (Washington, DC: International Resources Group and the U.S. Agency for International Development, Bureau for Africa, 1992), p. 40.
13. USAID, *Ecotourism*, p. 42.
14. USAID, *Ecotourism*, p. 44.
15. USAID, *Ecotourism*, p. 44.
16. Quoted from *New Frontiers* (Bangkok), March 1997, p. 1.
17. Jeffrey S. Marshall, "Papagayo Project Is Not Ecotourism," *Contours* (Bangkok) 7(8): 25.
18. Letter to author from Christophe Grenier, February 12, 1996, and subsequent discussions.
19. Sue Wheat, "Tourism: An Unwanted Guest?" *Tibet News* (London) 20 (1996): 4.
20. Brandon, *Ecotourism*, p. 53.
21. "Golf Courses Threaten Food Security," *Nation*, November 14, 1996.
22. "TAT's 'Sustainable Tourism' Policy Full of Contradictions," *New Frontiers*, (Bangkok), 1997, pp. 6 and 8.
23. Luciano Minerbi, "A Framework for Alternative and Responsible Tourism: Eco-cultural Tourism," paper presented at the Hawaii State Conference on Ecotourism, Honolulu, HI, September 26, 1994.
24. Biodiversity Conservation Network, "Ecotourism in the Rain Forest of Western Java," in *Biodiversity Conservation Network (BCN) 1996 Annual Report* (Washington, DC: Biodiversity Conservation Network and World Wildlife Fund, 1997), p. 18. BCN is a consortium of the World Wildlife Fund, the Nature Conservancy, and World Resources Institute and is funded by USAID and the United States–Asia Environmental Partnership.
25. Marcel Jansen, Jan W. Te Kloeze, and Han van der Voet, *Wakacje Na Wsi: Agritourism in Southwest Poland* (Wageningen, Netherlands: Center for

Recreation and Tourism Studies, Agricultural University, 1996).

26. Zac Goldsmith, "Eco-tourism: Old Wine—New Bottle?" paper presented at the Oko Himal Sustainable Tourism Conference, Kathmandu, Nepal, December 1996. Available from International Society for Ecology and Culture, Bristol, United Kingdom.

6

rethinking tourism

"**W**elcome to Paradise. . . . before it's gone" is indeed a macabre sales pitch. But current high-consumption forms of tourism are unsustainable. There is an urgent need for both tools and more realistic information. As travelers and members of our own communities, we need to look at root causes of global destruction and ask ourselves, "Why are we traveling? How can we change this destructive industry? Have there been any real changes?"

I recently asked these questions of several responsible tourism advocates. Virginia Hadsell, founder of the Center for Responsible Tourism, told me that despite the efforts of the worldwide responsible tourism movement since the 1970s, tourism's effects have worsened. But she sees some hopeful signs and believes "the issue of irresponsible tourism has been placed on the global agenda—at least in the U.S. tourism media—and the rate of the increase of abusing peoples, cultures, and environments has been slowed."

Over the past few decades, the world has truly shrunk, in a large part because of tourism. As citizens of the global North, we can fly to Rio de Janeiro tomorrow and float down the Amazon the day after. Our ability to see the world close up has made us more concerned about international problems. News about environmental threats to the rain forests, the plight of the people who live there, human rights abuses around the world, and the increasing poverty and economic gaps between citizens reach us speedily each day. Issues like the uncontrolled political power of transnational corporations and the destruction of the planet have become central in many of our lives. Yet in some ways the rapid rate at

117

which information is being thrown at us makes it almost too much to comprehend. We feel overwhelmed, sometimes jaded, by the surplus of information. We see the problems but remain unsure how to effect change.

Numerous "alternative" types of tourism are evolving, and the real danger is that travelers will simply consume these new products, places, and peoples without recognizing the urgent need for a critical reevaluation of global tourism and their participation in it. To rethink tourism is to challenge the travel industry at every level, including the booming new forms of travel, which, even if well intended, have many of the same detrimental effects as conventional tourism. Olivier Pouillon, a tourism activist who works in Indonesia, warns, "Stop looking for alternatives or technical solutions to tourism. When you scream ecotourism, agri-tourism, and alternative tourism, it makes people forget to look at what is wrong with *tourism*." Tourism scholar and activist Shelley Attix asks,

> Why are we "activists" afraid of the "t" word? Tourism industry peo-ple aren't. If we are concerned about what tourism is doing and come from different backgrounds—business, Indigenous sover-eignty, environmental—then we should talk instead of waiting until there is a crisis. It is very difficult, except in strategic boycott situa-tions, to shut down tourism. We have to keep alliances strong and prepare for transitional efforts. We need to train young people to be managers and handle policy decisions during these transitions from mass tourism. We have to make plans in terms of finances and man-agement skills to take over the helm and make big changes. We're making the "t" word so bad that no one wants to talk about it, and that's counterproductive.

The remedy is within tourism itself. To counter tourism's economic, social, and environmental devastation, we must learn to recognize cor-porate tourism's messages and methods. Tourism has provided us with fantasies. At the same time, it provides potentially free public relations that may help to encourage rethinking of the industry and create alter-natives. Tourism provides people-to-people contacts and an opportunity to utilize the ability to communicate with one another, to meet, and to organize. On a global level, this can help foster an appreciation for rich human, cultural, and ecological diversity and can cultivate a mutual trust and respect for one another and for the dignity of the natural world.

You and I are tourists, even if we are traveling to learn about or change the world. Unless we are willing to stay at home, reject the transportation systems, communication lines, and technologies and the tremendous amount of resources that we consume each time we travel, we need to understand not only our participation in the promotion of the global tourism industry but also its importance and potential as a tool for change. Tourism can raise awareness of and action for the global nature of problems like poverty, pollution, and cultural erosion. Close human relationships and activities liberated from preoccupations with profits and bottom lines are crucial to this awareness. In the past three decades, there has been a return to social responsibility and social idealism. This value shift is reflected to a small degree in the tourism industry (in the tourism-for-peace movement, for example) in the consciousness of the cross-cultural impact a travel experience has for both a visitor and the communities visited. The trend in travel is for more tourists and locals in alliance with schools, NGOs, religious groups, the media, cities, and governments to work to stop the paving of paradise.

So where do we start? With ourselves. We can read, learn, make personal changes, be more involved in our own communities, pressure governments and corporations, denounce exploitation, change policies, and investigate the global forces transforming our lives. We can discuss, educate, and organize. I believe that most tourists understand that there are many things wrong with tourism. What we need is a clear outline for change.

The first requirement is for more tourism research and analysis. This can occur as activism goes forward. Travelers from the global North can link with people in other places to make progress on issues that concern us all. By building on experiences and developing relationships and networks, we can challenge international trade and tourism policies, misinformation produced by the travel industry, and exploitative practices. We can make sure that monies from tourism go to the local economy.

Many developing countries are on the brink of abandoning traditional organic practices and moving toward more capital-intensive methods of development. The responsible tourism movement can draw attention to development policies that are undemocratic and promote reliance on the global economy as opposed to local resources. In many places around the world people are building sustainable communities that focus on the well-being of the community, rely more on renewable energy, discourage consumption, and create less pollution.

the need for education

While there has been a fair amount of critical analysis of tourism from the academic community, most tourism education focuses on hospitality management, training, and operations. Critical studies in economics, political control, culture, the North-South dichotomy, and the way tourists view themselves have contributed important insights. But real changes in tourism will not be created until people from diverse communities, backgrounds, and disciplines take a more integrated approach. Anthropologists, political scientists, and sociologists must connect with tourism management and training programs to share information.

Women of all colors are urgently needed to look at gender issues in tourism and change policies that exploit, discriminate, and cause violence to women. Support for tourism gender studies at universities and colleges will support education for women to work in tourism in areas other than as prostitutes, waitresses, maids, bar attendants, and housekeepers.

There needs to be tremendous support for Native and Indigenous students of tourism. While it is necessary to understand Western systems in order to tackle the issues of tourism, it is important to remember that Western education has produced the systems that are threatening the planet. Educational programs must introduce and integrate lessons from Indigenous ecological values and traditional and subsistence economics. I encourage students reading this book to research tourism, to undertake an analysis of advertising strategies or investigate the corporate responsibility of a tourism company. When educational programs encourage critical thinking and opportunities for people from diverse perspectives, they can create the tools, information, and education for those who are affected to change tourism. The global tourism industry must be persuaded to set aside some of its trillions of dollars in profits to advance the education of young people around the world to rethink tourism.

tourists as activists

The following tourism code was published in the *New Internationalist*.[1]

Caution:

Before Booking Your Holiday Ask Yourself
the Following Questions —
Which the Industry Is Not Keen to Answer

- What's the environmental impact of tourism on the country I want to visit? (e.g., reduction in water available for local population)
- Are people forcibly resettled to make way for tourist developments? (land clearance or local people banned from nature parks)

- By traveling to this country, am I supporting a repressive regime?
- Are the jobs created low skills, service-sector, and seasonal?
- Are my tastes increasing demands for goods/services from the North? ("I want to eat what I can get at home")
- Am I booked onto a national airline from the South?
- How is my presence influencing young people? (children lured away from education into selling tourist trinkets)
- Am I horrified by the "beggars and the poverty," or will I understand more about the North-South divide if I go? ("It makes me realize how lucky I am." "Why can't they run their society like ours?")
- How much have my attitudes to a culture/society been changed by the experience of being there? ("I came to escape all of the above. Where's the beach?")

The Center for Responsible Tourism suggests tourists ask themselves: Is this trip necessary? "Tourism has become a supermarket of illusions, exotic lands promising to satisfy secret desires. Ask yourself, why am I buying this trip? What do I leave behind? How many trips does it take to renew my soul and body? What do I do with my experiences when I return home?"[2] As tourists questioning tourism, the role we play, and the impact of our very presence in destination communities, we can start by considering the amount of natural resources it takes to transport us to our destination, to get us around while we are there (whether the oil used by airplanes and cars or the energy for the lights and air conditioning in the hotel room), where our waste is going, whether the locals have adequate water resources, how much land has been "reconstructed" for the place we stay, and whether residents have been moved to make room for us. Who owns the hotels, and where do our dollars go? We tourists can make some powerful political choices by voting with our feet and our pocketbooks.

As tourists, we must make educated economic choices and support small-scale, locally owned and operated businesses. Get involved in your own community so that when you travel you will have a reason to be involved in other communities and will *stay involved*; acknowledge the modern realities of Indigenous and rural communities and learn to respect, not romanticize, other cultures. Support responsible tourism organizations. Subscribe to their magazines and newsletters. Volunteer. Study. Learn about local currency programs and how you can start one in your community. Pressure large tourism companies to do more than greenwash. Organize a "reality tour" of your own community to examine environmental, economic, or social justice issues. Invite teachers, students, local community members, your family, city officials, religious leaders, local businesses (including those in tourism) and others to participate. Make activism a goal of the tour. Contribute funds to support more integrated, diverse critical tourism studies.

Travelers can act responsibly by seeking out accurate information about the places they intend to visit. In the United States and elsewhere, many Indigenous organizations will provide a list of recommended readings by authors they believe accurately describe their culture and history. Environmental and social justice groups that work with Native and Indigenous Peoples will have information about important current issues. Indigenous Peoples face any number of issues, ranging from health care and uranium mining cleanup to sovereignty rights and free trade agreements. In the United States, travelers can support the Native American Cultural Protection and Free Exercise of Religion Act, which guarantees protection of sacred religious sites and is the work of the Senate Indian Affairs Committee, the American Indian Religious Freedom Coalition, and hundreds of native communities all over the United States.

Most likely there are Indigenous Peoples in your community, a nearby community, or your state. Get involved with assessments of the impact of tourism around those areas. Bahe Rock, a Navajo and rethinking tourism activist, says, "People, especially young people, are naive. That is the first thing to realize and be aware of. If they realize that and admit it to themselves, it is the first step toward becoming a real human being. Then they should use their heads and their hearts to look for answers." Support Indigenous organizations working with the United Nations and other international institutions on biodiversity issues and policies. Tourism issues are part of their agenda to protect biodiversity and their environments.

While social activists are developing new tourism strategies, concerned tourists are changing their focus from relaxation to activism. Global Exchange, a San Francisco organization, has been a leader in people-to-people tourism. Their reality tours explore grassroots movements, offering travelers an opportunity to meet people behind the scenes, from Zapatistas in Chiapas and young people in Cuba to women organizers in South Africa and Vietnamese facing injustices created by capitalism. Tourists are now monitoring elections in Mexico, speaking out on behalf of Indigenous Peoples being forced from their lands by oil companies, and trying to uphold human rights in Bosnia. They are sharing information about fair trade, organic farming or permaculture, and less-consumptive technologies.

Deborah Tull joined a reality tour organized by Bard College:

I spent nine months traveling, meeting local people and helping out. I still have questions about what we did—did it really make a difference? Some places I could see that yes, it did. However, in other places I felt we were contributing to problems. Yet, overall, we traveled in a different way—meeting and learning from local people involved in important issues. It certainly changed my perceptions about tourism. It actually changed my life. I will never see tourism in the same light, I will never travel in a conventional way. I've talked to a lot of friends, family, and my teachers about it and believe I have been influential.

travel industry changes

Some segments of the travel industry are more aware of environmental and human rights issues and are actively involved in reform. A growing number of small tour operators are rethinking their industry. Although many alternative ideas claim to benefit local people, we must not lose sight of the fact that tour operators are in the business to make money, and the tourist is the paying consumer they cater to. Tourism researcher Barbara Johnson warns against some tourism ideas that are emerging:

Alternative tourism represents an industry whose ventures capitalize on the increasing global concern with disappearing cultures, lifestyles and ecosystems. . . . [However], the vision of responsible tourism includes more than this potentially exploitative relationship. Responsible tourism encompasses those ventures that are consciously designed to enhance the socio-environmental milieu of the host while educating and entertaining the guest. These ventures sell the "exotic" to gain money, labor, and/or foreign presence—all in an effort to restore the degraded environment while attacking the roots of social inequity.[3]

Many ecotourism projects are extremely misleading and exploitative. Some may be well intentioned but are misguided attempts to sell nature and culture. One example of a tour company that not only follows responsible tourism guidelines but also monitors the global travel industry is The Travel Specialists (TTS). A member of Co-Op America, a fair-trade organization, TTS serves as a link between concerned travelers, tour operators, tour programs, and local community projects. It evaluates other travel programs, promotes responsible tourism, and monitors the impact of tourism on local communities and the environment. TTS is involved in its own community in Massachusetts and has established the Eagle Eye Institute, a program to get urban youth out of the cities and into nature for hands-on learning experiences. The group also publishes a newsletter that includes travel opportunities, suggested readings on responsible tourism, and updates about the travel industry.

Pax World Tours demonstrates a commitment to peacemaking by facilitating citizen education and the flow of information and ideas through travel. Pax believes travel to be an important tool for increasing awareness about global issues and often works directly with civic groups to help strengthen internal bonds, clarify positions, and spur action. It organizes tours to areas of the world caught up in conflict, particularly where the conflict involves the United States. In 1992 former senator Charles Percy and John Anderson led a Pax tour to the Middle East. The group, including rabbis, Christian clergy, and Muslims; Jews, Anglos, and Arabs visited Israeli occupied territories, Syria, Jordan, and Egypt. It was the first time the Syrian president had received an American rabbi. Tour members also met with the king of Jordan, the Israeli prime minister, and members of the Palestinian leadership. After a Middle East agreement was signed at the White House, the group hosted a peace dinner for the same world leaders. Pax director Larry Ekin remarked, "I can't say how our tour helped the negotiations, but the goals articulated by the participants on tour closely resembled the settlement that was eventually negotiated. It has to send a message to leaders of peace and reconciliation in the Middle East when you have this type of diverse group agreeing on those principles." Said Ekin, "We are fighting an uphill battle against a gigantic travel-tour industry that simply wants to move the most people in the shortest period of time for maximum profit. For most of the travel industry, people-to-people travel just gets in the way of maximizing profits. We believe our programs have helped increase the scope of citizen democracy, refined its practice, and helped people understand that this is a legitimate and vital part of peacemaking."

more natural experiences

The real argument for environmental protection through any form of tourism requires a departure from the global marketplace economy that exploits the natural world. It is almost impossible to do this within the context of the global tourism industry, which gobbles up resources. We must expect to pay for the environments we visit. In the global North, we pay taxes to keep up our sewer systems, water, and even national parks. In many other countries, there is no such public support. If you plan to travel, factor in the cost of the environment and public services into your trip. Better yet, set aside funds especially for this purpose and donate them to an environmental organization or community development project. But it is important to understand as well that Western solutions to saving the planet are not always compatible with those of the people who live in wilderness areas. For example, conservation—a Western concept—is an idea that land should be preserved in its natural state. Under conservation statutes new parks, wildlife refuges, wilderness areas, and monuments have become protected lands. The designation of wilderness lands may actually impinge on Indigenous ways of life because limitations are placed on traditional and subsistence activities. Instead of developing new sites, new destinations, we should consider the pressing issues related to tourism that are already on our doorstep, investigate the "corridors" and peripheral areas of protected lands.

local action

Local people in destination communities are speaking out and taking action against exploitative tourism. Some paint murals on walls near tourist resorts to graphically illustrate their antitourism sentiments. Others have developed educational programs for residents and designed regional tourism strategies to protect their natural resources and limit the numbers of tourists and developers who enter their lands. Still others are setting up their own travel companies that promote responsible tourism through people-to-people links, some of which focus on human rights; they are developing tour programs that recruit scientists and volunteers to work directly with them to preserve their environments. Native people are taking over operations of parks—their ancestral homelands—and training others to do the same. While they share the use of these areas with tourists, their own communities are the first priority. They are establishing local currencies that keep dollars within the communities. Some are working with universities and local governments to come up with new policies on land planning and use in their regions. Some programs are even assessing the reasons *why* record numbers of stressed tourists are escaping from urban environments. Many programs examine the impacts of tourism upon their environments, teach tourists about the impact of their mere presence, and invite them to take action to help offset the damage. There are even projects for individuals or organizations in the United States and Europe to help purchase land in the global South to set aside as protected areas for wildlife and for local people.

Indigenous Peoples are resisting tourism with increasing strength. The Masai in Africa, the Mayans in Chiapas, the Quechuas in the Amazon, many Native people in the U.S., and many others are resisting irrational development of their lands in the name of ecotourism. These groups have organized opposition both from within their own countries and in the international community, and their voices are being heard. Responsible tourism groups, environmentalists, and others have responded by providing support and publicizing injustices. Concerned citizens rallied in 1996 to oppose the construction of a sprawling resort in the heart of India's Nagarhole National Park, one of the world's biological "hot spots" and home to Indigenous Peoples. The opponents denounced the development, organized locally with tribal people, and called upon responsible tourism organizations around the world to help publicize their plight. In 1997 the Indian courts ruled against the resort, at least for the time being.

Craig Chatman believes that people who live in tourist destinations must track how tourism dollars enter and leave their communities. His community is looking at the concept of local currency, originally conceived as Ithaca Hours in Ithaca, New York, in 1991 and now used in more than thirty communities throughout the United States and elsewhere. "Using a local currency means more dependency upon local resources," says Chatman. Community members who participate in the program offer skills or other goods they want to barter and sell; the money used to purchase these goods is pumped into the local economy and cannot leave. The idea is to encourage local spending and support neighbors and local resources instead of international imports.

It is essential to create links within communities. Foreign-owned or -operated tourism companies could help support local agriculture and more sustainable practices by buying local goods and services such as food and transportation. They could recognize the harm in building cluster sites and make sure broad planning in the area included agricultural lands and other lands used by locals.

the media

Most travel advertising of destination communities is created in the global North or by private industry and government tourist offices in the global

South. This medium dominates the planet and promises paradise while other sectors of the media discuss how backward, poor, and degraded these same locations are. Any argument to rethink tourism must see through this corporate vision and its methods of propaganda. While responsible tourism organizations and tourism scholars have provided the best critiques of global tourism, the mainstream media are taking notice, especially with the growing concern about threats to national parks and protected areas. More travel writers, newspapers, and magazines are responding to the alerts about negative tourism activities and providing more realistic accounts of the life of locals, the dismal conditions that tourism has helped create, and the antitourism campaigns launched by grassroots groups everywhere.

Clay Hubbs, an educator, started the alternative travel magazine *Transitions Abroad* in the mid-1970s to provide information on economical, purposeful international travel opportunities — travel that involves *learning* by living, studying, working, or vacationing alongside the people of the host country. Hubbs describes his magazine's mission:

> A lot of tourists have a consumer attitude — what can I get, instead of what can I learn. We have to put aside our own cultural biases and learn as much as possible from the people we visit. I find that if you stay long enough, learn the language, you get a sense of who locals are as "people." Through the magazine we are providing people-to-people links and small-scale programs, and with the numbers of people traveling "independently" mushrooming, it is obvious that people benefit and the travel industry does not.

Indigenous brochures describe cultural taboos and warn tourists from certain areas. Internet services speak to broad issues that affect both travelers and people in local destinations. Ron Mader, who coordinates the Internet service El Planeta Platica, told me, "It seemed to me that there were all of these groups not talking to each other about 'ecotourism.' I set up Planeta to run both positive and critical articles on ecotourism in the Americas and to hear from many people throughout the hemisphere. Many have been excluded from the governmental arena or the larger circles of powerhouse NGOs."

New and interesting media tools for tourists abound. One is *On This Spot: An Unconventional Map and Guide to Lhasa*, published by the International Campaign for Tibet. It provides uncensored stories behind Lhasa's tourist sites and commemorates dozens of places and events that the Chinese government is trying to hide from tourists and the international community. The map explains the contemporary political situation and gives the exact locations where Tibetan prisoners of conscience are held today. Linking travelers with Tibetan support organizations around the world, this map is a great example of a rethinking tourism tool.

What can you do to encourage the media and marketers to present a more realistic image of tourism and its effects? Don't buy travel magazines that are simply advertisements for corporations and reject the "awards" they give themselves. Support the alternative press that does not depend upon corporate funds and offers critical analysis of travel. Educate your local news media. As a tourist, researcher, or activist, you can write about your tourism experiences. Always make sure to include resource information to link people, and illustrate how the issues you learned about on your travels are related to you and your community. For example, a traveler to the Amazon wrote about irresponsible, exploitative oil and gas development and linked her story to increased consumer demand for petroleum in the United States.

human rights

On several occasions the United States has sought to use tourism as a political weapon. As Linda Richter, a tourism scholar who has researched politics and tourism in Asia, says, "The United States demonstrated opposition to the regimes of the People's Republic of China and Cuba by forbidding travel to those countries for many years. Now it is symptomatic of the desired change in political relationships that the United States has lifted the travel ban on the People's Republic of China (and) allowed some travel to Cuba."[4] By opening the doors of free trade, countries are "rewarded" with an expanding force of superconsumers, the tourists. They are also "rewarded" with expanding infrastructures, technologies, imports and exports, Western homogenization, and all the other tools of capitalism, consumerism, and globalization.

Despite the "rewards," some countries continue to oppress people. Individual tourists, as opposed to tour groups, have played a role in documenting some of the abuses simply by being part of the community. According to tourism analyst Ronald Schwartz, following demonstrations in Tibet in 1987, tourists who witnessed the events "became the principal source of information to journalists denied access to Tibet and gathered material on arrests, torture, and imprisonment for human rights organizations. A loosely knit network that arose in the first few days following the demonstrations continued to function for more than two years, recruiting new volunteers [tourists] to take the place of those who left."[5]

They also provided medical treatment to wounded Tibetans who were afraid to go to government hospitals. Yet Schwartz emphasizes that this was a special group of independent travelers who might have been concerned about human rights in Tibet in the first place. Such "engaged" tourists have not simply stepped out of their own societies, leaving behind obligations and seeking relaxation and luxury: "The ease with which travelers from different nationalities, a group of strangers, were able to create a clandestine organization and pool their skills . . . is remarkable. But their ready agreement on goals and tactics suggests a common culture of shared perceptions and values."[6] Engaged tourists share skills and values that belong to a larger social world.

monitoring corporations

Some corporations are taking steps to become more responsible, but only after facing tremendous pressure from the public. The public is needed to monitor and challenge corporations at every level. Community resistance to tourism corporations has been mostly unsuccessful. Nevertheless, resistance is increasing, and workers in the tourism industry are also organizing to resist. Any argument to rethink tourism calls for investigation of the power of international tourism corporations in order to get large corporations out of the local planning process and reduce their local political influence and control. In the United States, disclosure laws mean that information about global tourism corporations is fairly easy to obtain. The U.S. Securities and Exchange Commission requires corporations to file quarterly and annual reports. Any environmental liabilities—significant remediation or cleanup—must be reported. It is much more difficult to investigate overseas corporations. The best way is to locate and work with a grassroots group in the destination country. Friends of the Earth publishes the booklet *How to Research Corporations*. Other groups like the Multinational Monitor and Transnational Resource Action Center (TRAC) can also assist in investigating corporate actions and responsibility, and may help publish your own investigative work.

Travelers can learn more about corporate responsibility, oppressive governments, and actions against human rights abusers from the numerous publications that monitor human rights, corporations, the environment, and government actions. *Boycotts in Action* (BAN) provides information about boycotts of corporations, countries, and organizations, including tourism and travel-related corporations. A dedicated hiker told me, "People underestimate the power they wield. I became an environmental activist to save the places I love. It makes me angry to see politicians 'selling' wilderness areas, designing bills with loopholes allowing for construction of roads, power lines, and pipelines. I write about my experiences to encourage others to get involved. There is no doubt it is effective. Public pressure is the only way to make sure politicians don't sell out to private interests."

tourism revisited

In rethinking tourism, we must analyze the role we tourists play in promoting current destructive practices. With pressure, the industry can be reshaped so that profits from tourism are distributed more equitably. We must reduce consumption and respect natural limits rather than merely think "green." Technology is not neutral but interacts with society and nature. It is essential to replace environmentally and socially obsolete high technology with more appropriate, less-consuming, and traditional technologies.

This task is enormous. The developed world is in a state of denial about such severe problems. It is unlikely to change voluntarily; it will have to be forced by community groups in the global South and by cross-border organizations everywhere. A more generous spirit and greater volunteerism with respect to tourism issues goes hand in hand with a condemnation of the elitist, materialistic view that tourists are entitled to purchase other environments and cultures. Travelers must be willing to be on equal footing with locals, to try to understand cultures widely disparate from their own, to contribute to the community (perhaps through manual labor or professional expertise).

Those of us in the North who reject the advance of commercialized global culture and those from the South who are victimized by it vociferously oppose the continued devastation of the environment and Indigenous populations. We need to take a hard look at the travel industry, at the self-exploitation of communities, and the roles we play as individuals. This inner journey of reevaluation won't be easy, but it is essential.

Some say it is too late. At a conference to rethink current economic directions, a former executive of one of the largest travel companies in the world was asked if he could see an alternative future. He replied, "There is no way to stop economic globalization because tourism and travel have already created globalization." Yet because of global grassroots movements for change, it may be possible to develop a deeper under-

DEBORAH MCLAREN, LADAKH, INDIA

In an alternative tourism program, American and Ladakhi youth participate in a cultural exchange to examine development processes and common issues that affect them all.

standing of the course we're on and the role of global tourism. There *are* alternative strategies and movements, and there are alternatives *to* tourism.

Tourism has become politicized within global institutions, nations, communities, industry, the environment, and within almost all of us, whether we are tourists or persons affected by tourism in their community. The field begs for more research, monitoring, linking, policymaking, and change. Meanwhile, global tourism is growing at a phenomenal rate. There is an urgent need to rethink tourism and ecotravel and stop the paving of paradise.

It has been thirteen years since my trip to Jamaica. My continual journey through "tourism" over those years has been one of learning—sometimes frustrating, always challenging, often delightful, and in many ways transformative. When I think back to the day when I rode horseback among the shantytowns and hills near Montego Bay with Joseph, one thing seems clear to me: in many ways we were both searching for dignity and an opportunity for self-realization. Throughout the world, among different cultures and classes, people are looking for self-determination. The world we are now born into and the society we know measures humans in terms of their economic worth. Human potential is enormous and largely unrealized. Western-style capitalism and consumerism have undermined the possibility for people to make their own choices about their lives and to have opportunities for their futures. Tourism continues to play a tremendous role in spreading the corporate empire. However, it is an industry that is different from many others. One of its primary functions is to develop human relationships. I see that as a chance to rethink and change our future. *That* would be paradise.

notes

1. Quoted from a tourist caution in "Tourism—The Facts," *New Internationalist* (1993), p. 19.
2. Quoted from "Third World Travel—Buy Critically," brochure adapted from a TEN publication and distributed by the Center for Responsible Tourism, San Anselmo, CA.
3. Barbara Johnson, "Save Our Beach Dem and Our Land Too? The Problems of Tourism in America's Paradise," *Cultural Survival Quarterly* 14(2): 31.
4. Linda K. Richter, *The Politics of Tourism in Asia* (Honolulu: University of Hawaii Press, 1989), p. 6.
5. Ronald David Schwartz, "Travelers Under Fire: Tourists in the Tibetan Uprising," *Annals of Tourism Research* (New York: Pergamon Press, 1991), p. 588.
6. Schwartz, "Travelers," p. 589.

resources

this chapter is divided into sections
that list organizations directly or indirectly involved in rethinking tourism;
the final few sections consist of a more or less traditional bibliography.
Please note that many small, nonprofit groups cannot respond to blanket
requests for information, and they greatly appreciate contributions to
cover the costs of processing requests. In addition, readers are encouraged to share information with the organizations. The author and pub-
lisher do not endorse the organizations listed throughout this directory.
Readers are encouraged to investigate resources. Updates should be sent
to the author, care of the Rethinking Tourism Project, 1761 Willard St.,
NW, Washington, DC 20009.

These resources are listed under the following categories:
- Rethinking Tourism Groups
- Ecotourism Organizations
- Environmental and Development Organizations
- Green Hotels
- Indigenous Organizations
- U.S.-Based Responsible Tour Operators and Programs
- Social and Environmental Justice Programs (Tours, Delegations,
    Volunteer Programs)
- Human Rights and Social Justice Organizations (Information Only)
- Short-Term Travel Study Programs
- Tourism-Specific College and University Programs

- U.S. Government Contacts
- International Organization Contacts
- Magazines, Newsletters, Journals, Surveys, and Travel Guides
- Pamphlets, Maps, and Teacher's Aids
- Audiovisuals
- Books
- Guides for Students
- Web Sites

rethinking tourism groups

Alaska Wilderness Recreation and Tourism Association (AWRTA), PO Box 22827, Juneau, AK 99802; (907) 463-3038, fax (907) 835-3280, awrta@alaska.net. Promotes the protection of Alaska's wild places through communication, education, and political action, including the Dollar a Day Conservation Program.

Annapurna Conservation Area Project (ACAP), ACAP Headquarters Ghandruk, Ghandruk Panchayat, Kaski District, Nepal. Uses trekkers' fees to protect the environment and culture in north central Nepal.

Asia-Pacific Peoples' Environment Network (APPEN), 27 Lorong Maktab, 10250 Penang, Malaysia; 60-422-76930, fax 60-4227-5705. A regional anti-golf-course and environmental network.

Asia Tourism Action Network (ANTENNA), 15 Soi Soonvijai 8, New Petchburi Road, Bangkok, 10310, Thailand. Promotes locally controlled tourism; publishes a newsletter.

Asian Women's Association, Sakuragaoka, Shibuyaku, Tokyo 155, Japan; 81-3-346-9752. Affiliated with the Japanese Men's Group Against Prostitution in Asia; antiprostitution organization; promotes responsible tourism.

Badri Dev Pande, Environmental Education and Awareness, PO Box 3923, Kathmandu, Nepal; fax 9771-521-506. Developing a sustainable tourism master plan of Manaslu region of Nepal.

Broken Bud, 1765-D Le Roy, Berkeley, CA 94709; (510) 843-5506. Advocacy for antiprostitution tourism and child trafficking; newsletter.

Caribbean Conference of Churches, PO Box 616, Bridgetown, Barbados; fax (809) 429-2075. The new address of the Ecumenical Coalition on Third World Tourism (ECTWT).

Center for the Advancement of Responsible Travel (CART), 70 Dry Hill Park Road, Tonbridge, Kent TN10 3BX UK. Center of information on responsible tourism in Europe.

Center for Responsible Tourism, PO Box 827, San Anselmo, CA 94979; (415) 258-6594, fax (415) 454-2493. Publications, reports, newsletter, advocacy.

Center for Seafarers Rights, 50 Broadway, 3rd Floor, New York, NY 10004; (212) 269-2710. Documentation about workers on cruise ships; publications.

Coalition of Organizations for Solidarity Tourism, Postal Box 1172, Attn: PH c/o Philcom, 8755 Paseo de Roxas, Makati 1200, Philippines. Alternative tourism in the Philippines.

Coalition on Child Prostitution and Tourism, Christian Aid, PO Box 100, London SE1 7RT, UK. Responsible tourism group; antiprostitution tourism advocacy network.

Community Action International Alliance (CAIA), 110 Maryland Avenue, NE, Suite 504, Washington, DC 20002; (202) 547-2640, fax (202) 547-3136. Organizes environmental justice tours of Washington, DC; workshops, publications.

COOPRENA (National Eco-Agricultural Cooperative Network of Costa Rica), Aptdo. 6939-1000 San Jose, Costa Rica; (506) 225-1942, fax (506) 225-1942, camese@sol.racsa.co.cr. Consortium of cooperatives developing eco-agro tourism to relocalize and diversify tourism, conserve resources, and support small farms.

Ecumenical Coalition on Third World Tourism (ECTWT), PO Box 616, Bridgetown, Barbados; fax (809) 429-2075, contours@caribnet.net; Asia office: Box 35, Senanikhom, Bangkok 10902, Thailand; 662-939-7111, fax 662-939-7112, Contours@ksc.net.th. Organizes conferences; publishes *Contours* magazine, other resources.

End Child Prostitution in Asian Tourism (ECPAT) — Thailand, 328 Phayatai Road, Bangkok, 10400, Thailand; 662-215-3388, fax 662-215-8272; ECPAT — Canada, 11 Madison Avenue, Toronto, Canada M5R 2S2; (416) 323-9726, ecpat@globalpassage.com; ECPAT-USA, 475 Riverside Drive, Room 621, New York, NY 10115; (212) 870-2427, fax (212) 870-2055. An international campaign to end child prostitution and trafficking; educates tourists, the tourism industry, and governments about prostitution tourism.

EQUATIONS: Equitable Tourism Options, No. 198, II Cross, Church Road (Behind old KEB Office), New Thippasandra, Bangalore 560 075, India; 9180-528-2313; fax 9180-528-2313, admin@equations.ilban.ernet.in. Responsible tourism advocacy; helps travelers locate environmentally and culturally sensitive projects in India.

Euroter, 82, rue François Rolland, F 94130 Nogent-sur-Marne, France; (331) 4514-6421, fax (331) 439-49144. Publishes principles for developing green tourism in European villages.

Friends of Malae Kahana, PO Box 305, Laie, HI 96762; (808) 293-1736, fax (808) 293-2066. Native Hawaiian civic group operates state park; provides training to other native groups to manage parks.

Friends of PRONATURA, 240 East Limberlost Drive, Tucson, AZ 85705; (602) 887-1188, closfree@aol.com. Network of ecological groups working in Mexico.

Friends of the Earth (Amigos de la Terra), Tourism Campaign, c/o San Bernando 24, 3, 28015 Madrid, Spain; 34-71-301-492 or 34-71-307-110, foespain@nodo50. gn.apc.org. Research and networking on tourism industry activities and impacts.

GAG'M: Global Anti-Golf Movement and Global Network for Anti-Golf Course Action, 1047 Naka Kamogawa, Chiba, Japan 296-01; 81-47097-1001, fax 81-47097-1215. GAG'M, 27 Lorong Maktab, 10250 Penang, Malaysia; 604- 227-6930, fax 604-227-5705. Anti-golf initiative, work with grassroots and Indigenous groups throughout Asia and the Pacific displaced by golf development.

Global Exchange, 2017 Mission Street, San Francisco, CA 94110; (415) 255-7296, fax (415) 255-7698. Reality tours focus on public education about globalization issues and visit countries like South Africa, Haiti, Cuba, Mexico; publications.

Hawaiian Ecumenical Coalition on Tourism (HECOT), 766 North King Street, Honolulu, HI 96817; (808) 256-7218, fax (808) 843-0711. Research, activism, advocacy, publications.

Indonesian Resources and Information Program (IRIP), PO Box 190, Northcote 3070, Australia; 03-481-1581. Fosters active links with Indonesians working for change; publications.

International Bicycle Fund, 4887 Columbia Drive South, Seattle, WA 98108-1919; (206) 628-9314; intlbike@scn.org. Promotes bicycle transport, economic development, international understanding, and safety education; newsletter; links with other auto-free and bicycling organizations around the world.

International Institute for Peace Through Tourism, 3680 rue de la Montagne, Montreal, Quebec H3G 2A8, Canada; (514) 281-1822, fax (514) 848-1099. Facilitates tourism initiatives that contribute to international peace and cooperation.

Masai Environment Resource Center, 1025 Vermont Avenue, NW, Suite 300, Washington, DC 20005; (202) 783-7400. Promotes education and information about the threats to the Masai tribal people in Africa, including tourism and displacement.

NANET (North American Network for Ethical Travel), Office on Global Education, Church World Service, 2115 N. Charles Street, Baltimore, MD 21218-5755; (410) 727-6106, fax (410) 727-6108. Responsible travel group; education, advocacy, networking, data base of responsible tourism organizations.

North American Coordinating Center for Responsible Tourism, PO Box 827, San Anselmo, CA 94979; (415) 258-6594, fax (415) 454-2493. Newsletter, resource library, and publications.

Ökologischer Tourismus in Europa (OTE), Bernd Rath, Am Michaelshof 8-10, 53177 Bonn, Germany; 02-283-59008, fax 02-283-59096. Responsible tourism group.

Partners in Responsible Tourism, PO Box 419085-322, San Francisco CA 94141; (415) 273-1430, bapirt@aol.com. Primarily a network of representatives of tourism companies concerned about the impact of tourism on local environments and cultures and promotes cultural and environmental ethics and practices.

Responsible Tourism Network, PO Box 34, Rundle Mall, Adelaide, SA, Australia 5000; 618-232-2727, fax 618-232-2808, bwitty@ozemail.com.au. Responsible tourism in Pacific region; works with travel industry and tourism activists; pubishes responsible travel guide.

Rethinking Tourism Project, 1761 Willard Street, NW, Washington, DC 20009; (202) 797-1251, RTProject@aol.com. An educational and networking group for Indigenous Peoples.

Sahabat Alam Malaysia (Friends of the Earth Malaysia), 19 Kelawai Road, 10250 Penang, Malaysia; 04-376-930. Works on tourism issues.

Third World Tourism European Ecumenical Network (TEN), Nikolaus-Otto-Strasse 13, 70771 Leinfelden-Echterdingen, Germany; 7-11-7989-281, fax 7-11-7989-123. Responsible tourism.

Tourism Concern, Stapleton House, 277-281 Holloway Road, London N7 8HN, UK; 44-171-753-3330, fax 44-171-753-3331, tourconcern@gn.apc.org. Advocates, investigates, educates; publishes quarterly magazine. Videos, documentation, teaching resources.

Tourism Industry Development Council, 634 S. Spring Street, Suite 1016, Los Angeles, CA 90014; (213) 486-9880. Monitors environment and labor issues.

Tourism Investigation and Monitoring Team, c/o Towards Ecological Recovery and Regional Alliance (TERRA), 5th Floor, TVS Bldg., 509 Soi Rohitsook, Pracharat Bampen Road, Bangkok 10320, Thailand; 66-2-69107-1820, fax 66-2-6910-714. Investigates tourism development in the Mekon subregion; publications.

Tourism with Insight (Arbeitsgemeinschaft Tourismus mit Einsicht), Hadorter Strasse, trraper@ksc.net.th 9B, 8130 Starnberg, Germany. Responsible tourism study group.

Tourism Watch (ZEB/FFT), Nikolaus-Ottoo-Str. 13, 70771 Leinfelden-Echterdingen, Germany; 49-711-798-9281, fax 49-711-798-9283, dienste@geod. geonet.de. Coordinates a European network of responsible travel organizations.

Transverses, 7 rue Heyrault, F-92100 Boulogne, France; tel/fax 331-49-10-9084. Responsible tourism in Europe.

Wisnu Foundation, Jl. Muding Indah 1/1, Kerobokan, Denpasar 8117, Bali, Indonesia; tel/fax 62-0361-424-758. Concerned with environmental problems caused by tourism; works with small-scale, locally based enterprises; conducts environmental audits of resorts and hotels.

WorldViews, 462 19th Street, Oakland, CA 94612-2297; (510) 835-4692, fax (510) 835-3018, worldviews@igc.apc.org. Magazine, data resource center, and library; documentation on responsible tourism.

ecotourism organizations

Alternative Tour Thailand, 14/1 Soi Rajatapan, Rajaprarop Road, Tayathai, Bangkok 10400, Thailand; 66-2-245-2963. Supports environmental efforts of small communities throughout Thailand by organizing low-impact tours and homestays.

Belize Ecotourism Association, 195A Vista Del Mar, Ladyville, 025-2806, Belize; fax 501-252-598 or Belize Ecotourism Association, c/o Chaa Creek Lodge, San Ignacio Town, Cayo District, Belize. Membership ecotourism groups.

Bina Swadaya Tours, Jl. Gunung Sahari 111/7, Kakarta Pusat, PO Box 1456, Jakarta, 10014, Indonesia; 62-21-420-4022. Leaders in alternative community-developed tourism; helped establish the Indonesian Ecotourism Association.

Biodiversity Conservation Network, c/o World Wildlife Fund, 1250 24th Street, NW, Washington, DC 20037; (202) 861-8348, fax (202) 861-8324. Consortium of environmental organizations funded by USAID; funds ecotourism projects.

Conservation International, Ecotourism Department, 1015 18th Street, NW, Suite 1000, Washington, DC 20036; (202) 429-5660, fax (202) 887-0193. Develops ecotourism programs; assists community-based programs.

Ecotrans, Marcenado, 24-28002, Madrid, Spain; 34-1-413-9710, fax 34-1-416-1720. Tourism and environment information network; associated with planning and policy at the governmental level.

Ecotrans E.V., c/o Herbert Hamele, Adelgundenstrasse, 18, 80538 München, Germany; 44-892-95610, fax 44-892-92740. Ecotourism group in Germany; associated at the government level.

Ecotourism Association Australia, PO Box 130, Terrey Hills, NSW 2084, Australia; 02-486-3316, fax 02-486-3353. Membership ecotourism association; Aboriginal ecotourism.

The Ecotourism Society (TES), PO Box 755, North Bennington, VT 05257; (802) 447-2121, fax (802) 447-2122, ecotsocy@igc.apc.org. Dedicated to making tourism a viable tool for conservation and sustainable development; publications and videos; educational programs.

European Center for Eco-Agro Tourism, PO Box 10899, Amsterdam 1001 EW, Netherlands; 31-206-68-1030, fax 31-206-650-166, eceat@antenna.nl. Over 200 small farms are members of the network; feasibility studies, guides to farms; assists other countries to develop networks.

Hawaii Ecotourism Association, PO Box 61435, Honolulu, HI 96839; (808) 956-2866, fax (808) 956-2858, tabata@hawaii.edu. Promotes responsible tourism, resource network for Hawaii and the Pacific.

Indonesian Ecotourism Network (INDECON), Jalan H. Samali No. 51, Pejaten Barat, Pasar Minggu, Jakarta 12510, Indonesia; tel/fax 62-21-799-3955, indecon@cbn.net.id. Developing an ecotourism data base, information center, newsletter, manuals, guidebooks; conducts workshops, seminars.

Kodukant Ecotourism Initiative, SAARISOO, EE 3482 Joesuu, Parnumaa, Estonia; 372-446-6405, fax 372-444-3779. A network of small tour operators living in or nearby protected areas in rural settings; reference manual.

Pacific Rim Institute of Tourism, 930-555 West Hasting Street, Vancouver, BC V6B 4N6, Canada; (604) 682-8000, fax (604) 688-2554. Works in ecotourism.

Samoan Ecotourism Network (SEN), PO Box 4606, Matautu-utu, Western Samoa; 685-26-940, fax 685-25-993, ecotour@pactok.peg. apc.org. Concerned about deforestation of primary rain forests; organizes ecotours.

Sikkim Biodiversity and Ecotourism, Opp. Krishi Bhawan, PO Tadong, 737 102, Sikkim, India; tel/fax 91-3592-233-35. Developing regional ecotourism program with local communities in the Himalayas.

Talamanca Association for Ecotourism and Conservation (ATEC), Puerto Viejo de Talamanca, Limon, Costa Rica. Community group that promotes small, locally owned, socially responsible tourism businesses in Talamanca (Atlantic coast area). Local people are Bribri and Cabecar Indians and West Indian (Afro-Caribbean) immigrants.

Toledo Ecotourism Association (TEA), San Miguel Village, Toledo District, Belize; (501) 72-2119. Network of Indigenous farm cooperatives; requesting paying volunteers to help with their programs.

Turismo Ecologico y Cultural del Pueblo Maya, San Cristobal de las Casas, Chiapas, Mexico. An alternative ecotour group organized by Indigenous Peoples in Chiapas.

World Conference on Sustainable Tourism, Viana 50, 38201 La Laguna, Tenerife, Islas Canarias, Spain; 34-22-603-064, fax 34-22-603-074. Organizes global conferences on sustainable tourism.

environmental and development organizations

Alliance for a Paving Moratorium/Fossil Fuels Policy Action Institute, PO Box 4347, Arcata, CA 95521; (707) 826-7775, alliance@tidepool.com. Highways watchdog group; promotes restructuring of the American way of life away from growth, toward ecodemocracy. Publishes magazine.

Center for Clean Development, 1227 W. 10th Avenue, Eugene, OR 97402; (503) 346-0676, fax (503) 346-2040, ccd@igc.apc.org. Rethinking development, promoting systems for a better environment.

Chilean Ecological Action Network, Seminario 744 Nunoa, Santiago, Chile; 56-2-223-4483. Coalition of over 100 Chilean environmental, Indigenous, and social action organizations.

Community Baboon Sanctuary, Bermudian Landing, Belize District, Belize; 2-44-405 or 2-77-369. Developing conservation and ecotourism strategies.

Co-op America, 1612 K Street, NW, Suite 600, Washington, DC 20006; (202) 872-5307, fax (202) 331-8166, info@coopamerica.org. Membership group of businesses and cooperatives dedicated to creating a just and sustainable society by harnessing economic power for positive change. Publishes boycott information, alternative travel links, and magazine.

Council on Economic Priorities, 30 Irving Place, New York, NY 10003-2386; (212) 420-1133, fax (212) 420-0988; cep@echonyc.com. A nonprofit public service research organization dedicated to accurate and impartial analysis of the social and environmental records of corporations and bringing about reform.

Cousteau Society, Project Ocean Search, 930 W. 21st Street, Norfolk, VA 23517; (804) 627-1144. Marine guidelines and information about threats to the world's oceans.

Earth Island Institute, 300 Broadway, Suite 28, San Francisco, CA 94133-3312; (415) 788-3666. Publishes "How Green Is Your Tour: Questions to Ask Your Tour Operator"; turtle watch tours.

50 Years Is Enough–U.S. Network for Global Economic Justice, 1025 Vermont Avenue, NW, Suite 300, Washington, DC 20005; (202) 463-2265, fax (202) 879-3186, sb50years@igc.apc.org. Coalition working in partnership with grassroots movements in over fifty countries dedicated to realizing profound change at the World Bank. Some members work on tourism issues.

Friends of the Earth, 1025 Vermont Avenue, NW, Suite 300, Washington, DC 20005-6303; (202) 783-7400, fax (202) 783-0444. Researches, monitors corporations; publishes booklet "How to Research Corporations"; Spain office has tourism campaign. Also see Oceanic Society Expeditions (below).

Global Response, PO Box 7490, Boulder, CO 80306-7490; (303) 444-0306, fax (303) 449-9794; globresponse@igc.apc.org or http://www.globalresponse.org. Environmental action and education network.

Greenpeace Pacific Campaign, 568 Howard Street, 3rd Floor, San Francisco, CA 94105; fax (415) 512-8699. Information about ecotourism and alternative technologies.

Institute for Earth Education, PO Box 115, Cedar Cove, Greenville, WV 24945; (304) 832-6404, fax (304) 832-6077, ieei@aol.com. Professional organization for educators in the environmental field; conferences; free sourcebook.

Interhemispheric Resource Center, PO Box 4506, Albuquerque, NM 87196-4506; (505) 842-8288, fax (505) 246-1601, resourcectr@igc.apc.org. A research and policy center that produces popular education materials, policy reports, periodicals and books about current economic and political issues and promotes development that is participatory and environmentally sustainable.

International Forum on Globalization, 1555 Pacific Avenue, San Francisco, CA 94109; (415) 771-3394. Network of activists, students, organizations around the world to counter economic globalization; organizes global teach-ins. International Forum on Globalization-Europe, Canonbury Villas, London N1 2PN, UK; 44-171-359-3533, fax 44-171-696-0014. Organizing grassroots groups, NGOs, and students to rethink economic globalization and promote community self-reliance.

International Society for Ecology and Culture/Ladakh Project (ISEC), 21 Victoria Square, Clifton, Bristol BS8 4ES, UK; 44-1179-731-575, fax 44-1179-744-853. Educational campaigns on globalization issues, including tourism study groups; educational materials.

Kathmandu Environmental Education Project, Box 9178 Tridevi Marg, Thamel, Kathmandu, Nepal; 977-1-410-303, fax 977-1-411-533. Concerned about sustainable tourism issues, policies, planning in Nepal.

Ladakh Project, PO Box 9475, Berkeley, CA 94709; (510) 527-3873. Educational programs, resource materials on counterdevelopment, study groups, books, videos.

Land Trust Alliance, 1319 F Street, NW, Suite 501, Washington, DC 20004; (202) 638-4725. Publishes "Starting a Land Trust," a practical handbook that provides case studies and an extensive list of resources.

The Millennium Institute, 1117 N. 19th Street, Suite 900, Arlington, VA 22209; (703) 841-0048, fax (703) 841-0050, millennium@igc.apc.org, or http://www.igc. apc.org/millennium. Moving the world toward a peaceful, just and sustainable future using the energies of the turn of the millennium and quantitative analysis. Works with NGOs, U.N. agencies, development banks, national governments, and religious insitutions. Computer simulation models for sustainable development, reports; award-winning website includes tourism.

Mexican Action Network on Free Trade (RMALC), Godard No. 20, Col. Guadalupe Victoria 07790 Mexico, DF; 52-5-355-1177, rmalc@laneta.apc. Information about grassroots groups and NGOs in Mexico; some monitor tourism development.

Multinationals Resource Center, PO Box 19405, Washington, DC 20036; (202) 387-8030, fax (202) 234-5176, mrc@essential.org. Provides workers, environmental activists, consumer groups, and local journalists in less-industrialized countries with crucial information for their research and campaigns, specializes in information about U.S.-based multinational companies but can help answer a variety of environmental, consumer, and labor-related questions.

National Audubon Society, 700 Broadway, New York, NY 10003; (212) 979-3000, fax (212) 353-0347. Publishes travel ethics and coordinates a Golf Course Action program.

Nature Conservancy, 1815 N. Lynn Street, Arlington, VA 22209; (703) 841-5339, fax (703) 843-4880. Works to bring sustainable protection to natural areas. Ecotourism projects and other environmental protection programs throughout the world.

Rainforest Action Network, 450 Sansome Street, Suite 700, San Francisco, CA 94107; (415) 398-4404, fax (415) 398-2732. Promotes the preservation of the world's rain forests; publishes fact sheets, information on ecotourism.

RARE Center for Tropical Conservation, 1616 Walnut Street, Suite 911, Philadelphia, PA 19103; (215) 735-3510, fax (215) 735-3515, rare@igc.org. Assists communities in designing conservation programs, including ecotourism; trail and guide training programs and manuals.

Redefining Progress, One Kearny Street, 4th Floor, San Francisco, CA 94108; (415) 781-1191, fax (415) 781-1198. An activist think tank challenging conventional economics, provides alternatives to traditional models, including the "Genuine Progress Indicator" (GPI), a new model for communities and cities that accounts for the social and ecological costs of economic activities and ecological tax reform.

Rocky Mountain Institute, 1739 Snowmass Creek Road, Snowmass, CO 81654-9199; (970) 927-3851, fax (970) 927-3420. Redefining success in the energy and transportation sectors, publications include community handbooks and guides.

Save the Earth Foundation, 4881 Topanga Canyon Boulevard, Woodland Hills, CA 91364; (818) 883-2784, stearth@earthlink.net. Supports environmental research and education; funds generated through the promotion of Save the Earth products.

Sierra Club, 85 Second Street, 2nd Floor, San Francisco, CA 94105; (415) 977-5500. Dedicated to protection of the wilderness; education, advocacy, and publications. Sponsors ecotours and environmental outings from inner city to international. Books, magazine, other publications.

SOMO Centre for Research on Multinational Corporations, Keizersgracht 132, NL-1015 CW Amsterdam, Netherlands; 020-639-1291, fax 020-639-1321. Investigates multinational corporations.

Transnational Resource and Action Center (TRAC), PO Box 29344, San Francisco CA 94129; (415) 561-6568, fax (415) 561-6493, trac@igc.org. Works to build global links for social justice, ecological sustainability, and democratic control over corporations. TRAC hosts Corporate Watch (www.corpwatch.org), an online resource on transnational corporations.

Tread Lightly, 24th Street, Suite 325, Ogden, UT 84401; (801) 627-0077, fax (801) 721-8633. Dedicated to increasing awareness about damage from off-highway vehicles to public and private lands.

Trust for Public Lands, 116 New Montgomery, 4th Floor, San Francisco, CA 94105; (415) 495-4014. Works nationwide to conserve land for people; opposes irrational development of wild spaces.

Wilderness Society, 900 17th Street, NW, Washington, DC 20006; (202) 833-2300, fax (202) 429-3958. Information on national wilderness issues and grassroots groups around the country forming to protect them.

Wildlife Conservation International, PO Box 62844, Nairobi, Kenya; 254-2-21-699, fax 254- 2-15-969. Ecotourism; proceedings from 1992 Kenya ecotourism workshop.

Wildlife Preservation Trust International, 3400 Girard Avenue, Philadelphia, PA 19104-1196; (215) 222-3636, fax (215) 222-2191, WPTI@aol.com. Dedicated to the preservation of endangered species; supports research, education, and professional training programs. Tours are seen to be a positive connection for members interested in supporting endangered species.

World Resources Institute, 1709 New York Avenue, NW, Washington, DC 20006; (202) 638-6300, fax (202) 638-0036, info@wri.org. Policy research center assists governments, international organizations, and private businesses to address sustainable development, biodiversity protection, analysis of ecotourism programs.

World Wildlife Fund, 1250 24th Street, NW, Washington, DC 20037; (202) 293-4800, fax (202) 293-9211. Collaborates with environmental efforts in developing countries to design ecotourism projects and protected areas; offers travel programs to members.

green hotels

Green Hotels Association, PO Box 420212, Houston, TX 77242-0212; (713) 789-8889, fax (713) 789-9786. Has list of hotels around the world that are becoming green. (Investigate whether a "green" hotel in your community is "green" in another country.)

International Hotel Environment Initiative, The Prince of Wales Business Leaders Forum, 5 Cleveland Place, London SW1 6JI, UK; 44-171-321-6384, fax 41-171-321-6480. Associated with "green" ecotourism development projects around the world.

indigenous organizations

Most nonprofit Indigenous groups do not have tourism-specific programs, although they publish newsletters and magazines that cover tourism issues. Please send a contribution to cover the cost of information requests. Many tribes can be contacted through their tourism offices or through state tourism offices.

Abya Yala Fund, PO Box 28703, Oakland, CA 94604; (510) 763-6553. Indigenous organization established to obtain funds to promote Indigenous self-development; publications sometimes include tourism.

Amanaka'a, 60 East 13th Street, New York, NY 10003; (212) 253-9502. Organizes an annual "Amazon Week" to discuss and learn about issues affecting Indigenous Peoples in the Amazon, including tourism issues.

Amazon Coalition, 1511 K Street, NW, Suite 627, Washington, DC 20005; (202) 637-9718, fax (202) 637-9719, amazoncoal@igc.apc.org. Coalition of Amazonian and U.S. groups; publishes newsletter.

Cultural Survival Canada, 200 Isabella Street, Suite 304, Ottawa, Ontario K1S 0V7, Canada; (613) 237-5361, fax (613) 237-1547. An international Indigenous Peoples organization supports self-determination; sustainable economies; rights to cultural and environmental integrity, land, and resources. CSC also coordinates the Indigenous Peoples Biodiversity Network (IPBN).

First Nations Conferences, PO Box 1240 Station "M," Calgary, Alberta T2P 2L2, Canada; (403) 261-3022, fax (403) 261-5676. For information about Canadian aboriginal tourism.

First Nations Development Institute, The Stores Building, 11917 Main Street, Fredericksburg, VA 22408; (540) 371-5615. Dedicated to grassroots development for Native Americans. Supports some local sustainable tourism initiatives.

Hopi Tribe, Office of Public Relations, PO Box 123, Kykotsmovi, AZ 86039; (520) 734-2441, ext. 341. Information about tourism policy and visitor guidelines.

Indigenous Affairs, International Work Group, Flolstroede 10, DK-1171 Copenhagen, Denmark; 45-3312-4724, fax 45-3314-7749, iwgia@login. dknet.dk. An independent international organization to support indigenous people; magazines and publications available in English and Spanish.

Indigenous Environmental Network, PO Box 485, Bemidji, MN 56601; (218) 751-4967, fax (218) 751-0561, ien@igc.apc.org. Alliance of grassroots Indigenous Peoples whose mission is to protect the earth from contamination and exploitation by strengthening, maintaining, and respecting the traditional teachings and natural laws.

Indigenous Peoples Intellectual Property Rights Center, IPBN-IPR Centre, Mataatua Declaration Directorate, PO Box 13-177, Johnsonville, Wellington, Aotearoa, New Zealand; tel/fax 64-4-479-7781, aroham@nzonline.ac.nz. Research, advocacy in support of intellectual property rights (biodiversity, Indigenous knowledge).

Indigenous Peoples of East Africa Foundation, PO Box 59516, Nairobi, Kenya; 254-2-723-002. Information center for Indigenous organizations in East Africa.

Indigenous Women's Network, PO Box 174, Lake Elmo, MN 55042; (612) 777-3629. A network representing Indigenous women from the Americas and Pacific region, strengthening their community work through networks: rebuilding families, communities, and nations; magazine.

Native Lands Institute, 823 Gold Avenue, SW, Albuquerque, NM 87102; (505) 242-4020. Information and advocacy to protect Native lands and water resources; publications.

Rethinking Tourism Project, 1761 Willard Street, NW, Washington, DC 20009; (202) 797-1251, RTProject@aol.com. Indigenous education and networking on tourism issues.

South and Meso American Indian Rights Center (SAIIC), PO Box 28703, Oakland, CA 94604; (510) 834-4263, fax (510) 834-4264. Resource center on Central and South American Indigenous organizations; publishes magazine that covers development issues, including tourism.

South Pacific Peoples Foundation, 1921 Fernwood Road, Victoria, BC V85 2Y6, Canada; (604) 381-4131. Information about organizations, issues in South Pacific; magazine.

Survival for Tribal Peoples, International Secretariat, 11-15 Emerald Street, London WC1N 3A1, UK; 071-242-1411. Publishes information about tribal peoples and critical issues, including tourism impacts.

Survival International, 310 Edgeware Road, London, W2 1DY, UK; 071-723-5535, fax 071-723-4059, survival@gn.apc.org. Advocacy, information, education about survival for tribal peoples; concerned about tourism impacts.

u.s.-based responsible tour operators and programs

Appropriate Technology Tours, 1150 Janes Road, Medford, OR 97501; (541) 773-2435. Promotes alternative technologies through travel programs.

Baikal Reflections, Inc., PO Box 310, Mesa, CO 81643-0310; (970) 268-5885, fax (970) 268-5884, baikal@igc.apc.org. Offers programs to Siberia.

Eco-Travel Services, 5600 Miles Avenue, Oakland, CA 94618; (510) 655-4054, ecotravel@wonderlink.com. Nationwide individual and corporate travel arrangements, uses smaller operators; supports local economies and environmentally conscious operations instead of quick profits; publishes newsletter.

Environmental Travel, 119-66 80th Road, Kew Gardens, NY 11415; (800) 876-0048. Travel agency caters to needs of vegetarians, vegans, and animal rights advocates.

Himalayan High Treks, 241 Delores Street, San Francisco, CA 94103-2211; (800) 455-8735, fax (415) 861-2391, effie@well.com. A small trekking company that specializes in trips to Bhutan, India, Nepal, and Tibet; offers specialized programs for women; publishes newsletter.

Journeys International, 4011 Jackson Road, Ann Arbor, MI 48103; (313) 665-4407 or (800) 255-8735, fax (313) 665-2945, journeysmi@aol.com. A well-established ecotour operator; guides are either natives or residents of the countries they visit; part of their profits supports environmental preservation.

Oceanic Society Expeditions, Fort Mason Center, Bldg. E, San Francisco, CA 94123; (415) 441-1106, fax (415) 474-3395. Promotes environmental stewardship, education, and research through ecotourism.

Pax World Tours, 1111 16th Street, NW, Suite 120, Washington, DC 20036; (202) 293-7290, fax (202) 293-7023, paxworldsvc@aol.com. Works for peace and justice through initiating and supporting innovative programs that encourage peace-making and community-based development. Promotes people-to-people links and responsible tourism.

South American Explorer's Club (SAEC), 126 Indian Creek Road, Ithaca, NY 14850; (607) 277-0488, fax (607) 277-6122, explorer@samexplo.org. Hiking club promotes responsible tourism.

Tour de Cana, PO Box 7293, Philadelphia, PA 19101; (215) 222-1253. An outgrowth of the organization Bikes Not Bombs, this group offers bike trekking with a social, cultural, and political spin.

Travel Specialists, 120 Beacon Street, Somerville, MA 02143-4369; (617) 497-8151 or (800) 370-7400, ext. 51, fax (617) 492-3720. Evaluates travel programs, operators, and the travel industry; arranges alternative trips and programs around the world.

Travel Quest, 3250 Barham Boulevard, Los Angeles, CA 90068; (213) 876-3250, fax (213) 876-3295, 74732.3153@compuserve.com. Promotes greater care and understanding of the planet, people, and other beings.

Yukon River Tours, 214 Second Street, Fairbanks AK 99701-4811; (907) 452-7162. Educational ecotours; learn about Athabascan culture at a Native fish camp on the Yukon river.

Wilderness Travel, 801 Allston Way, Berkeley CA 94710; (510) 548-0420, fax (510) 548-0347, info@wildernesstravel.com. Promotes cultural preservation and environmental protection; supports conservation, cultural, and development organizations.

Wildland Adventures, Inc., 3516 NE 155th Street, Seattle, WA 98155; (800) 345-4453, (206) 365-0686, fax (206) 363-6615, wildadve@aol.com. Ecotour operator offers group travel, customized trips for independent travelers and families, rain forest workshops, and responsible trips like trail cleanups and community services. Contributes part of profits to conservation and community development at the local level.

social and environmental justice programs (tours, delegations, volunteer programs)

American Friends Service Committee, 1501 Cherry Street, Philadelphia, PA 19102; (215) 241-7000. Volunteer programs to community projects in Mexico and Cuba.

Bangladesh Workcamps Association, 289/2 Work Camps Road, North Shahjahanpur, Dhaka 17, Bangladesh; fax 882-86-3797. Links to short-term and medium-term volunteer work camp projects throughout Bangladesh.

Centro Felix Varela, Aptdo. 4841 Plaza, Ciudad Habana 10400, Cuba. Devoted to international peace and cooperation, ecologically responsible societies, seminars, exchanges, humanitarian donations, publications, video production, special reports.

Conflict Resolution Catalysts, PO Box 836, Montpelier, VT 05601; (802) 229-1165. Volunteers participate in conflict resolution programs in communities in countries like Bosnia-Herzegovina (works with the United Nations High Commissioner for Refugees). Helping children deal with trauma of war.

Cuba Information Project, 198 Broadway, Suite 800, New York, NY 10038; (212) 227-3422. Cosponsors social justice delegations.

Earthwatch, 680 Mount Auburn Street, Watertown, MA 02272; (617) 926-8200, fax (617) 924-7100. Voluntary scientific international tours; magazine.

Ecumenical Program of Central America and the Caribbean (EPICA), 1470 Irving Street, NW, Washington, DC 20010; (202) 332-0292, fax (202) 332-1184, epica@igc.apc.org. A small press and solidarity group working on social justice issues, speaking tours, delegations.

Farm Helpers in New Zealand, Kumeroa Lodge, RD1, Woodville, New Zealand 5473; 64-6-376-4582. Members link to farmers looking for helpers in exchange for room and board.

Foreign Placements, PO Box 912, Somerset West 7129, South Africa; 27-4457-7677. Volunteer programs in South Africa for those with medical and other skills.

Global Citizens Network, 1931 Inglehart Avenue, St. Paul, MN 55104; (612) 644-0960. Volunteer programs to rural Kenya.

Leave No Trace, 288 Main Street, Lander, WY 82502; (307) 332-8880, fax (307) 332-8811. Teaches skills to hikers, backpackers, and horsepackers for protecting wilderness areas.

Native Forest Network Environmental Justice Tours, Native Forest Network, PO Box 57, Burlington, VT 05402; (802) 863-0571. Organizes research and fact-finding expeditions to learn about and publicize Indigenous issues of development and gain understanding of Indigenous issues in Central America.

Operations Crossroads Africa, 475 Riverside Drive, Suite 830, New York, NY 10027; (212) 870-2106. Projects in rural Africa staffed by self-financing volunteers.

Pastors for Peace, 1607 West Winnemac Avenue, Chicago, IL 60640; (773) 271-5269. Volunteer caravans of trucks bring material aid to Chiapas, Mexico, and Guatemala.

Peace Brigades International, 2642 College Avenue, Berkeley, CA 94704; (510) 540-0749. Through peace programs and delegations, volunteers link with Indigenous and other rural people.

Sea Turtle Research Expeditions, Sea Turtle Restoration Project, 300 Broadway, Suite 28, San Francisco, CA 94133; (800) 859-SAVE, earthisland@igc.apc.org. Volunteers participate in one- and two-week biological and conservation projects in Costa Rica and Mexico.

Traveler's Earth Repair Network (TERN), PO Box 4469, Bellingham, WA 98227; (360) 738-4972, fax (360) 671-9668. Links travelers with people and organizations working in restoration, sustainable agriculture, and environmental issues; lists over 100 countries.

Voluntarios Solidarios, 995 Market Street, Suite 801, San Francisco, CA 94103; (415) 495-6334. Places U.S. volunteers with Latin America and Caribbean peace and justice grassroots groups for service between three months and two years. Also sponsors occasional human rights and peace and justice delegations.

WWOOF (Working for Organic Growers), 19 Bradford Road, Lewes, Sussex BN7 1RB, UK. WWOOF, Mt. Murrindal Cooperative, Burchan, Victoria 3885, Australia; 61-5-155-0218. 400 member farms and volunteer opportunities. Connects members with organic farmers throughout the world.

Youth Charitable Organization, 20/14 Urban Bank Street, Yellamanchili, 531055 Visakhapatnam District, Andhra Pradesh, India; 91-8-924-51122. Volunteers for local community and ecological work.

human rights and social justice organizations (information only)

Asia Pacific Center for Justice and Peace, 110 Maryland Avenue, NE, Box 70, Washington, DC 20002; (202) 543-1094, fax (202) 546-5103, apcip@igc.apc.org. Network of community groups, social justice groups, and grassroots organizations.

Australia West Papua Association, PO Box 65, Millers Point, NSW 2000, Australia. West Papua Action Kit: suggestions for action, resources, maps, on tourism, human rights, refugees, deforestation, mines, dams, resistance movements.

Human Rights Watch, 485 Fifth Avenue, New York, NY 10017-6104; (212) 972-8400, fax (212) 972-0905. Information on human rights in specific countries such as Burma and Tibet.

International Campaign for Tibet, 1825 K Street, NW, Suite 520, Washington, DC 20006; (202) 785-1515, fax (202) 785-4343. Publishes "On This Spot: An Unconventional Map and Guide to Lhasa."

National Coalition Government of the Union of Burma, 815 15th Street, NW, Suite 910, Washington, DC 20005; (202) 393-7342, fax (202) 393-7343. Burma Action Group-UK, Collins Studios, Collins Yard, Islington Green, London N1 2XU, UK; (171) 359-7679; fax (171) 354-3987, bagp@gn.apc.org. Australia Burma Council, PO Box 2024, Queanbeyan NSW, Australia 2620; (616) 297 7734, fax (616) 297 7773, azappia@spirit.com.au. Opposes tourism to Burma under current oppressive government; publications available.

National Labor Committee, 275 7th Avenue, New York, NY 10001; (212) 242-3002, fax (212) 242-3821. NLC supports worker and human rights. Publications; educational campaign about workers' rights.

Open Society Institute-Burma Project, 888 7th Avenue, New York, NY 10106; (212) 887-0632. Information about anti-tourism campaign.

Third World Network, 228 Macalister Road, Penang, Malaysia; (604) 373-511. Produces a magazine and other information about development issues in the global South, including tourism.

Free-Tibet Campaign, 9 Islington Green, London, N1 2XH, UK; 0171-359-7573, fax 0171-354-1026. Independent membership organization campaigning for the rights of Tibetan people. Publishes magazine; reports on tourism in Tibet.

short-term travel study programs

American University Study Tour, World Capitals Programs, Dublane House-Tenley Campus, American University, Washington, DC 20016-8080; (202) 895-4900. Offers programs on both the United States and other countries on global policy issues.

Center for Alternative Technology, Education Office, Machynlleth, Powys, Wales SY20 9AZ; 44-1654- 703-743, fax 44-1654-702-782. Residential courses at a learning center dedicated to exploring renewable technologies; individual, group, and family vacations.

Center for Global Education, Augsburg College, 2211 Riverside Avenue, Minneapolis, MN 55454; (800) 299-8889 or (612) 330-1159, fax (612) 330-1695, globaled@augsburg.edu. Organizes tours to the global South to learn about social and environmental issues.

Council on International Educational Exchange, 205 East 42nd Street, New York, NY 10017; (212) 661-1414. International work programs for students.

Global Awareness Through Experience (GATE) 912 Mark Street, La Crosse, WI 54601; (608) 791-5283. Student programs throughout the world.

Institute for Central American Development Studies (ICADS), Field Course in Resource Management and Sustainable Development, ICADS, Dept. 826, PO Box 025216, Miami, FL 33102-5216; icadscr@expreso.com. Interdisciplinary semester focusing on development issues from ecological to socioeconomic perspectives.

Our Developing World, 13004 Paseo Presada, Saratoga, CA 94070-4125; (408) 379-4431. Educational project to bring Third World realities to North Americans. Community programs, teacher training and materials, resource library, study tours.

School for Field Studies, 16 Broadway, Beverly, MA 01915-4499; (508) 927-7777. International field studies and hands-on opportunities for high school and college students concerned about the environment.

School for International Training, PO Box 676, Kipling Road, Brattleboro, VT 05302-0676; (800) 336-1616, fax (802) 258-3500, csa.sit@worldlearning.org. The summer abroad training concentrates on experiential learning, homestays, intensive language instruction, and independent study projects.

Taking Off, PO Box 104, Newton Highlands, MA 02161; (617) 630-1606. Assists university students to volunteer in projects overseas.

University Research Expeditions Program (UREP), University of California-Berkeley, Berkeley, CA 94720-7050; (510) 642-6586, fax (510) 642-6791, urep @university.berkeley.edu. Scientific, voluntary environmental travel study programs; participants assist researchers on programs such as tracking monkeys in the rain forests and pelicans in the Sea of Cortez; supports community-based ecotourism programs.

VIEW Foundation, 13 Hazelton Avenue, Toronto, Ontario M5R 2E1, Canada; (416) 964-1914, fax (416) 964-3416. Educational ecotour programs for young people to Central America and Antarctica.

tourism-specific college and university programs

East-West Center, 1777 East-West Road, Honolulu, HI 96848; (808) 944-7271. Affiliated with the University of Hawaii; special expertise in tourism assessment.

Faulkner State Community College, Travel/Tourism Management, Baldwin County and Alabama Gulf Coast College, 3301 Gulf Shores Parkway, Bay Minette, AL 36507-2698; (334) 986-3104. Undergraduate program in ecotourism.

George Washington University, International Institute for Tourism Studies, 817 23rd Street, NW, Bldg. K, Washington, DC 20052; (202) 994-7087, fax (202) 994-1420. Programs in international tourism studies. Offers undergraduate and graduate programs.

Goddard College, Institute for Social Ecology, PO Box 89, Plainfield VT 05667; (802) 454-8493. Travel study programs; individually designed programs allow students to take on critical tourism studies.

Griffith University Gold Coast, International Center for Ecotourism Research, PMB 50, Gold Coast 4215, Queensland, Australia; 61-75-948-668, fax 61-75-948-679. Ecotourism studies.

Indiana University, RHIT Dept., 799 W. Michigan, Indianapolis, IN 46202; (317) 274-2599, fax (317) 274-4567. Undergraduate tourism programs.

Institute of Eco-Tourism, Srinakkarinwirot University-Patumwan Campus, Henri-Dunant Road, Bangkok 10330, Thailand; 66-2-252-27044, fax 66-2-254-4599. Graduate programs, research.

International Honors Program in cooperation with Bard College, 19 Braddock Park, Boston, MA 02116; (617) 267-0026, fax (617) 262-9299. Nine-month global ecology program takes students to meet activists and progressive thinkers, grassroots organizations. Focuses on cultural anthropology, sustainability, and the environment.

Kodolanyi Janos College, Tourism Department, Szabadsagmarcos U59, Iranyi Daniel u.4. 8000, Szekesfehervar, Hungary; 22-316-123, fax 22-331-237. Undergraduate studies.

North Carolina State, Sustainable Tourism Programs, Box 7344, Raleigh, NC 27695-7344; (919) 515-2087. Undergraduate programs.

Trent University, Department of Geography, Box 4800, Peterborough, Ontario, Canada, K9J 7B8; (705) 748-1426, fax (705) 748-1205, fhelleiner@trentu.ca. Sustainable tourism studies.

University of Alaska–Fairbanks, School of Management, PO Box 756080, Fairbanks, AK 99775-7080; (907) 474-7211. Programs through the international tourism program and the Alaska Institute of Tourism.

University of Hawaii at Manoa, Honolulu, HI 96822; (808) 956-8111. Tourism management, urban and regional land planning, other programs involving tourism research and studies.

University of New Hampshire, Department of Resource Economics and Development, 310 James Hall, Durham, NH 03824-3589; (603) 862-1234. Compiled report "University Based Education and Training Programs in Ecotourism or Nature-Based Tourism in the USA."

University of Oregon, Micronesia and South Pacific Program, 5244 University of Oregon, Eugene, OR 97403-5244; (503) 346-3815. Program for sustainable communities studies and tourism development in Micronesia and the South Pacific.

University of Wisconsin–Stout, Hospitality and Tourism, Menomonie, WI 54751; (715) 232-2339, fax (715) 232-3200, jafari@uwstout.edu. Publishers of the *Annals of Tourism Research*.

u.s. government contacts

Designations to U.S. National Wilderness Preservation System require congressional approval, and agency management decisions involving public lands are open to public comment. For wilderness legislation updates contact the Sierra Club Legislative Hotline (202) 675-2394 or http://www.sierraclub.org.

Commerce Department, 14th & Constitution Avenue, NW, Washington, DC 20004. U.S. Travel and Tourism Administration (202) 482-2404; International Economic Policy (202) 482-3022; International Trade Development (202) 482-1461.

Interior Department, 1849 C Street, NW, Washington, DC 20240. For administrative decisions affecting U.S. protected lands. Bureau of Indian Affairs Tourism Office (202) 208-3710; President's Council on Sustainable Development (202) 408-5296; Territorial and International Affairs (202) 208-6816.

National Park Service, Department of Interior, Box 37127, Washington, DC 20013; (202) 208-6843. For information about national parks wilderness study area information, national parks, wildlife refuges, and Bureau of Land Management administrative decisions.

No Sweat, Department of Labor, Washington, DC 20210; fax (202) 219-8740; http://www.dol.gov/dol/nosweat.htm. Information about companies in the tourism industry that exploit laborers.

State Department, 2201 C Street, NW, Washington, DC 20010. Tourism Office (202) 647-4196.

U.S. Agency for International Development, 2201 C Street, NW, Washington, DC 20523; (202) 647-4000.

U.S. Forest Service, Cultural and Heritage Tourism, 324 25th Street, Ogden, UT 84401; (801) 625-5172, fax (801) 625-5170. Contact for U.S. Forest Service eco-tourism information, publications, planning.

U.S. Forest Service, Department of Agriculture, Box 96090, Washington, DC 20090; (202) 205-0957. Information about U.S. Forest Service wilderness study areas. Each state has designated tourism staff.

international organization contacts

National Center for Infectious Disease Control, Centers for Disease Control and Prevention, International Travel, 1600 Clifton Road NE, Mail Stop E03, Atlanta, GA 30333; (888) 232-3228 or (404) 639-3311. Information on health and disease around the world.

World Bank, Public Information Center (PIC), 1818 H Street, NW, Washington, DC 20433; (202) 458-5454, fax (202) 522-1500, pic@worldbank.org; http://www. worldbank.org. The PIC is open to the public and handles requests for specific documents on specific projects; they do not take blanket requests for information.

World Tourism Organization, Calle Capitan Haya, 42, 28020 Madrid, Spain; 01-571-0628, fax 01-571-0757, omt@dial.eunet.es. World tourism statistics, planning, policy, publications.

World Travel & Tourism Council, 20 Grosvenor Place, London SW1X 7TT, UK; 44-171-838-9400, fax 44-171-838-9050. Council of travel industry CEOs; research, reports, publications.

magazines, newsletters, journals, surveys, and travel guides

Abya Yala News: A Journal of the South and Meso American Indian Rights Center, SAIIC, PO Box 28703, Oakland, CA 94604; (510) 834-4263, fax (510) 834-4264. Covers development issues for Indigenous Peoples, including tourism.

Alaska Wilderness Recreation and Tourism Association Newsletter and *Directory,* published by AWRTA, PO Box 22827, Juneau, AK 99802; (907) 463-3038, fax (907) 463-3280. Updates on environmental issues related to tourism in Alaska; directory of ecotour operators.

Alternative Press Index, The Alternative Press Center, PO Box 33109, Baltimore, MD 21218; (410) 243-2471, fax (410) 235-532, altpress@igc.apc.org. Quarterly index to alternative and radical publications.

ANLetter: Equations Quarterly on Third World Tourism, Critique and Responses, Equitable Tourism Options. Distributed in the United States by the Center for Responsible Tourism, PO Box 827, San Anselmo, CA 94979; (415) 258-6594, fax (415) 454-2493. Articles, network news, news reports, list of resources, book reviews.

Auto-Free Times, Alliance for a Paving Moratorium, Fossil Fuels Policy Action Institute, PO Box 4347, Arcata, CA 95518; (707) 826-7775, fax (707) 822-7007, autofree@tidepool.com. Dedicated to fighting road construction through revolutionary ecology and economics.

Boycott Action News, sponsored by Co-op America, 1612 K Street, NW, Suite 600, Washington, DC 20006; (202) 872-5307. Updates on boycotts on countries and corporations.

Boycott Quarterly, Center for Economic Democracy, PO Box 30727, Seattle, WA 98103-0727; boycottguy@aol.com. News and updates on boycotts.

Contours: Concern for Tourism, Ecumenical Coalition on Third World Tourism, PO Box 35 Senanikhom, Bangkok 10902 Thailand; 66-2-939-7111, fax 66-2-939-7112, Contours@ksc.net.th. Quarterly magazine; news from developing countries.

Co-Op America Quarterly, 1612 K Street, NW, Suite 600, Washington, DC 20006; (202) 872-5307. Covers emerging ideas and models for creating a just and sustainable society, including travel companies and responsible tourism.

Costa Rica Outlook, Away from It All Press, PO Box 5573, Chula Vista, CA 91912-5573; (619) 421-6602. Updates on ecotourism in Costa Rica.

Cultural Survival Quarterly, Cultural Survival, 46 Brattle Street, Cambridge, MA 02138; (617) 441-5400, fax (617) 441-5417, csinc@cs.org. Back issues include "Breaking Out of the Tourist Trap" 14 (1 and 2); ongoing coverage of tourism impacts.

E: *The Environmental Magazine*, Earth Action Network, PO Box 4098, Westport, CT 06881; (203) 854-5559. Covers some environmental travel issues, see November-December 1996 issue.

Earth Island Journal, Earth Island Institute, 300 Broadway, Suite 28, San Francisco, CA 94133-3312; (415) 788-3666, fax (415) 788-7324. Some environmental tourism issues.

The Ecologist, Hogarth House, 32-34 Paradise Road, Richmond, Surrey TW9 1SE, UK; 44-181-332-6963. Information on globalization issues, voices from the global South.

Ecotourism and Hawaii's Visitor Industry, Research and Economic Analysis Division, Department of Business, Economic Development and Tourism, Mauka Tower, 737 Bishop Street, Suite 1900, Honolulu, HI 96813; (808) 586-2466. Quarterly report.

EcoTraveler, 2535 NW Upshur Street, Portland, OR 97210; (503) 224-9080, fax (503) 224-4266. Provides latest updates on ecotourism.

Foghorn Press, 555 De Haro Street, The Boiler Room #220, San Francisco, CA 94107; (415) 241-9550, fax (415) 241-9648. Outdoor and recreation books.

Frommer's Travel Guides, Macmillan Travel, 1633 Broadway, New York, NY 10019, or Frommer's Travel Book Club, PO Box 473, Mt. Morris, IL 61054-0473; (815) 734-1104. Travel guides.

Greenmoney Journal, 608 W. Glass Avenue, Spokane, WA 99205; (509) 328-1741. A socially responsible investing, business, and consumer resource; past issues include ecotravel.

Indigenous Affairs: The Indigenous World, Indigenous Affairs, International Work Group, Flolstroede 10, DK-1171 Copenhagen, Denmark; 45-3312-4724, fax 45-3314-7749. English and Spanish.

Indigenous Woman, Indigenous Women's Network, PO Box 174, Lake Elmo, MN 55042. Quarterly magazine; some coverage of tourism impacts on Indigenous Peoples.

Indochina Spotlight: Tourism and Tourism-Related Developments in Cambodia, Laos, and Vietnam, ECTWT, PO Box 35, Senanikhom, Bangkok 10902, Thailand. Newspaper and magazine clippings.

In Focus, Tourism Concern, Stapleton House, 277-281 Holloway Road, London N7 8HN, UK; 44-171-753-3330, fax 44-171-753-3331, tourconcern@gn.apc.org. Magazine for Tourism Concern members and others.

In These Times: The Alternative Newsmagazine, Institute for Public Affairs, 2040 N. Milwaukee Avenue, Chicago, IL 60647; (312) 772-0100. See special "Bummer Vacations Issue," July 1994.

John Muir Publications, PO Box 613, Santa Fe, NM 87504; (505) 982-4078. "Adventures in Nature" travel guide series.

Journal of Sustainable Tourism. Clevedon: Channel View Books/ Multilingual Matters Ltd., Frankfort Lodge, annual.

Ladakh Project Newsletter, ISEC, PO Box 9475, Berkeley, CA 94709; (510) 527-3873; in England contact ISEC/Ladakh Project, 21 Victoria Square, Clifton, Bristol BS8 4ES, England.

Lonely Planet Guides, Lonely Planet Publications, PO Box 2001A, Berkeley, CA 94702; (510) 893-8555, fax (510) 893-8563 or PO Box 617, Hawthorne, Vic 3122, Australia. For Lonely Planet travel guides.

Moon Travel Handbooks, Moon Travel Publications, PO Box 3040, Chico, CA 95927; (800) 345-5473. Travel guides.

Multinational Monitor, PO Box 19405, Washington, DC 20036; (202) 387-8030. Monthly newsmagazine dedicated to tracking and exposing illegal, abusive, and deceptive activities of multinational corporations.

New Frontiers Newsletter, c/o Tourism Investigation and Monitoring Team, TERRA, 5th Floor, TVS Bldg., 409 Soi Rohitsook, Prachrat Bampen Road, Bangkok 10320, Thailand; 66-2-69-107-1820, fax 66-2-69-7910-714, terraper@ksc. net.th. Excellent monitoring of tourism in Mekong subregion.

New Internationalist, PO Box 1143, Lewiston, NY 14092; (416) 257-4626. Employee cooperative producing monthly magazine on Third World development; tourism issues included.

Newsletter of the Center for Responsible Tourism, PO Box 827, San Anselmo, CA 94979; (415) 258-6594, fax (415) 454-2493. Tourism issues, articles, and poems from local people in destinations around the world; reviews new resources and books on tourism.

Planet Talk, Lonely Planet Publications, 155 Filbert Street, Suite 251, Oakland, CA 94607; info@lonelyplanet.com.

El Planeta Platica, c/o Talking Planet, http://www.planeta.com. The on-line newsletter of Latin American ecotourism.

Responsible Tourism: A Resource Guide, WorldViews and ECTWT, 462 19th Street, Oakland, CA 94612-2297; (510) 835-4692, fax (510) 835-3018. worldviews @igc.apc.org. A compilation of resources on global tourism.

Sierra Club Adventure Travel Guides, Sierra Club Books, 730 Polk Street, San Francisco, CA 94109; (805) 965-3452. For "Adventuring In . . ." travel guide series.

Survival for Tribal Peoples, Survival International, 11-15 Emerald Street, London WC1N 3QL, UK; 44-171-242-1441. Newsletter for Survival International members.

Tranet (Transnational Network), PO Box 567, Rangeley, ME 04907; (207) 864-2252. Bimonthly newsletter by and for people participating in the social paradigm shift in all parts of the world. Numerous responsible tourism contacts, projects, ideas.

Transitions Abroad: The Guide to Learning, Living, and Working Overseas, Transitions Abroad, 18 Hulst Road, PO Box 344, Amherst, MA 01004; (415) 256-3414. An education-oriented travel magazine that pioneered socially and ecologically responsible tourism writing.

Utne Reader, PO Box 7460, Red Oak, IA 51591-0460; (800) 736-8863. The best collection of viewpoints from the alternative press.

Voice of the Turtle Newsletter, Turtle Island Office, 4035 Ryan Road, Blue Mounds, WI 53517; (608) 767-3931, beabriggs@aol.com. From the organizers of the first bioregional gathering in the Americas in Mexico.

World of Work, International Labor Organization, Washington Branch, 1828 L Street, NW, Suite 801, Washington, DC 20036; (202) 653-7652. Quarterly magazine includes information on child labor, tourism labor.

WorldViews Magazine, c/o The Data Center, 464 19th Street, Oakland, CA 94612-2297; (510) 835-4692, worldviews@igc.apc.org. Formerly Third World Resources, this group has a public-access library, a quarterly magazine, and search-and-document delivery services.

pamphlets, maps, and teacher's aids

Agenda 21 and Tourism, Tourism Concern, Stapleton House, 277-281 Holloway Road, London N7 8HN, UK; 44-171-753-3330, fax 44-171-753-3331, tourconcern @gn.apc.org.

Ashton Ray E., Applied Technology and Management, 2770 NW 43rd Street, Gainesville, FL 32606, Compilation of his ecotourism-related articles.

Ecotourism Guide, Tasmanian Greens, Craclair Tours, PO Box 516, Devonport 7310, Australia; (614) 24-7838, fax (614) 24-9215.

"Ecotourism: Suicide or Development?" Ole Kamuaro, *Voices From Africa #6: Sustainable Development*, UN Non-Governmental Liaison Service, Room 6015, 866 United Nations Plaza, New York, NY 10017.

Golf and Tourism in Thailand, by Anita Pleumaron. Research report available from Tourism Concern, Stapleton House, 277-281 Holloway Road, London N7 8HN, UK; 44-171-753-3330, fax 44-171-753-3331, tourconcern@gn.apc.org.

Indigenous Peoples and Global Tourism, Rethinking Tourism Project, 1761 Willard Street, NW, Washington, DC 20009.

Indochina Spotlight: Tourism and Tourism-Related Developments in Cambodia, Laos, and Vietnam. ECTWT, PO Box 35, Senanikhom, Bangkok 10902, Thailand.

On This Spot: An Unconventional Map and Guide to Lhasa (Tibet), International Campaign for Tibet, 1825 K Street, NW, Suite 520, Washington, DC 20006; (202) 785-1515, fax (202) 785-4343. Uncensored stories behind Lhasa's tourist sites; explains contemporary human rights and political situations and shows the exact locations where Tibetan prisoners of conscience are held.

Responsible Tourism: A Hawaiian Point of View, Hawaii Ecumenical Coalition on Tourism, 4504 Kukui Street, Suite 16, New Pacific House, Kapa'a, HI 96746; (808) 822-7444. Responsible tourism fact sheet and recommendations.

Sustainable Tourism: Checklist for Responsible Tour Operators, International Bicycle Fund, 4887 Columbia Drive South, Seattle, WA 98108-1919; (206) 628-9314. Checklist covers operations and itineraries for cultural sensitivity, environmental impact, economic benefits.

Tourism and Indigenous Peoples: A Resource Guide, ECTWT, PO Box 35, Senanikhom Bangkok 10902, Thailand; 7-72-939-7111, fax 662-939-7112, contours @comnet.ksc.net.th.

Tourism — Paradise in Peril: Facts Have Faces, NANET, 2115 N. Charles Street, Baltimore, MD 21218-5755; (410) 727-6106. Fact sheet on tourism's cultural costs.

Towards Sustainable Tourism: The Experience of Wales, by R. Elwyn Owens, Wales Tourist Board, Brunel House, 2 Fitzalan Road, Cardiff, Wales, CF2 1UY, UK; 442-224-9909, fax 442-22-48-5031.

audiovisuals

Ancient Futures: Learning From Ladakh, Ladakh Project, PO Box 9475, Berkeley, CA 94709; (510) 527-3873. Available in several languages.

Bull Frog Films, PO Box 149, Oley, PA 19547; (800) 543-3764, bullfrog@igc. apc.org. Videos for rent or purchase include *Haida Gwaii — The Queen Charlotte Islands in the Web of Life*, produced by Barbara Barde, depicting tourism and Indigenous Peoples in Canada, and *Yosemite and the Fate of the Earth*, produced by the Yosemite Guardian Project of Earth Island Institute, depicting the impact of development around the world and its effect on wildlife.

Central Television Enterprises, Hesketh House, 43-45 Portman Square, London W1H 9FG. Tourism films include *Thailand for Sale*, produced by David Jay and coproduced by Small World Productions.

Interlock Media/Environmental Media Unit, 607 Boylston Street, 4th Floor, Boston, MA 02116; (617) 236-4471, fax (617) 236-4429, intlock@ix.netcom.com. Informational and training films and videos on Indigenous rights, environmental movements, domestic and Third World.

Living Media, produced by Peter Wirth and Chris Bolt, Write G/W Associates, 702 S. Beech, Syracuse, NY 13210. (315) 476-3396. $9.99 plus $1.50 for postage. This is a 60-minute audiocassette tape designed to give people who travel to the Third World the skills and confidence to use the media to share that experience.

Planning an Excellent Adventure. Ecumenical Exchange Office. Worldwide Ministries Division, Presbyterian Distribution Service. (800) 524-2612. 20 minute video offers a guide for groups planning trips.

Tourism Concern, Stapleton House, 277-281 Holloway Road, London N7 8HN, UK; 44-171-753-3330, fax 44-171-753-3331, tourconcern@gn.apc.org. Videos and films for rent or purchase include *Cannibal Tours* by Dennis O'Rourke (Australia, 1987); *Señor Turista*, by Gertrude Bohm (Germany/ Peru, 1983/1985); *Our Man In . . . (Goa, Cuba, Kenya); Tourism in Zimbabwe; Tourism in Mountain Areas*; young people's programs. Many are also available on audiotape.

books

Ashworth, G. J., and A. G. J. Dietvorst, eds. *Tourism and Spatial Transformations.* Wallingford, Oxford: CAB International, 1995.

Attix, Shelley A., ed. *Ecotourism: A Directory of Marketing Resources.* Pearl City: University of Hawaii, 1993.

Badger, A., P. Barnett, L. Corbyn, and J. Keefe. *Trading Places: Tourism as Trade.* London: Tourism Concern, 1996.

Barke, M., J. Towner, and M. T. Newton, eds. *Tourism in Spain.* Wallingford, Oxford: CAB International, 1996.

Barnet, Richard J., and Ronald E. Muller. *Global Reach: The Power of the Multinational Corporations.* New York: Simon and Schuster, 1974.

Barry, Tom. *The Other Side of Paradise: Foreign Control in the Caribbean.* New York: Grove Press, 1984.

Benjamin, Medea, and Andrea Freedman. *Bridging the Global Gap.* Cabin John, MD: Seven Locks Press, 1988.

Berger, Thomas R. *Village Journey: The Report of the Alaska Native Review Commission.* New York: Hill and Wang, 1985.

Berrigan, Tom. *The Travel Industry Environmental Sourcebook: A Project of the Responsible Tourism Initiative.* Washington, DC: Travel Association of America, 1994.

Black, Maggie. *In the Twilight Zone: Child Workers in the Hotel, Tourism and Catering Industry.* Geneva: International Labor Organization, 1995.

Blake, Beatrice, and Anne Becher. *The New Key to Costa Rica*, 13th edition. Berkeley: Ulysses Press, 1997.

Boissevien, Jeremy, ed. *Coping with Tourists: European Reactions to Mass Tourism.* Oxford: Bergharn Books, 1996.

Boo, Elizabeth. *Ecotourism: The Potentials and Pitfalls.* Washington, DC: World Wildlife Fund, 1989.

Brandon, Katrina. *Ecotourism and Conservation: A Review of Key Issues.* Washington, DC: World Bank, 1996.

Brause, Diane. *Directory of Alternative Travel Resources.* Dexter, OR: Lost Valley Educational Center, 1996.

Briguglio, Lino. *Sustainable Tourism in Islands and Small States.* London: Pinter, 1996.

Bureau of Tourism Research. *Tourism and the Environment.* Canberra, Australia: Bureau of Tourism Research, 1992.

Burns, Peter. *Tourism: A New Perspective.* Englewood Cliffs, NJ: Prentice-Hall, 1995.

Bushnell, Sherry. *The Ecotourism Planning Kit: A Business Guide for Ecotourism Operators in the Pacific Islands.* Honolulu: University of Hawaii, 1994.

———. *Pacific Islands Ecotourism: A Business Planning Guide.* Honolulu: Pacific Business Center Program, University of Hawaii, 1991.

Buzzworm. *Earth Journal 1993: Environmental Almanac and Resource Directory.* Boulder, CO: Buzzworm Books, 1993.

Cater, Erlet, and Gwen Lawman, eds. *Ecotourism: A Sustainable Option?* New York: John Wiley, 1994.

Ceballos-Lascarain, Hector. *Tourism, Ecotourism, and Protected Areas: The State of Nature-based Tourism Around the World and Guidelines for Its Development.* North Bennington, VT: The World Conservation Union and Ecotourism Society, 1996.

Centers for Disease Contol. *Health Information for International Travel.* Atlanta: Centers for Disease Control, 1994.

Christian Aid. *Abuse of Innocence: Tourism and Child Prostitution in the Third World*, London: Christian Aid, 1995.

Chopra, Suhita. *Tourism and Development in India.* London: Ashish Publishing House, 1991.

Cooper, Christopher P. *Tourism and Hospitality Education.* Guildford: University of Surrey, 1994.

Crossette, Barbara. *So Close to Heaven: The Vanishing Buddhist Kingdoms of the Himalayas.* New York: Alfred A. Knopf, 1995.

Cultural Survival. *State of the World's Indigenous Peoples.* Cambridge: Cultural Survival, 1993.

Danaher, Kevin. *Beyond Safaris: A Guide to Building People-to-People Ties with Africa.* Trenton, NJ: Africa World Press, 1991.

de Kadt, Emanuel, ed. *Tourism: Passport to Development? Perspectives on the Social and Cultural Effects of Tourism in Developing Countries.* London: Oxford University Press, 1978.

Durning, Alan Thein. *Guardians of the Land: Indigenous Peoples and the Health of the Earth*. Washington, DC: World Watch Institute, 1994.

Eber, Shirley, ed. *Beyond the Green Horizon: Principles for Sustainable Tourism*. London: Tourism Concern/World Wildlife Fund, 1992.

Ecotourism Society. *Ecotourism: An Annotated Bibliography for Planners and Managers*. North Bennington, VT: Ecotourism Society, 1993.

Ecumenical Coalition on Third World Tourism (ECTWT). *Caught in Modern Slavery*. Bangkok: ECTWT, 1992.

———. *Tourism: An Ecumenical Concern: The Story of the Ecumenical Coalition on Third World Tourism*. Bangkok: ECTWT, 1988.

———. *Tourism and Indigenous Peoples: A Resource Guide*. Bangkok: ECTWT, 1995.

———. *Tourism Prostitution Development Documentation*. Bangkok: ECTWT, 1983.

——— and Center for Responsible Tourism (CRT). *Alternative Tourism: A Resource Book*. San Anselmo, CA: ECTWT-Bangkok and CRT-Berkeley, 1990.

End Child Prostitution in Asian Tourism (ECPAT). *Children in Prostitution: Victims of Tourism in Asia*. Bangkok: ECPAT, 1994.

English, E. Philip. *The Great Escape? An Examination of North-South Tourism*. Ottawa: North-South Institute, 1986.

Fillmore, Mary. *Suggested Guidelines for Assessment of the Impacts of Tourism on Women*. Bangalore: Equations, 1994.

Forsyth, Tim. *Sustainable Tourism: Moving from Theory to Practice*. London: Tourism Concern and World Wildlife Fund, 1996.

Friendship Press. *Having an Excellent Adventure: A Handbook for Responsible Travel—A Guide for Planners and Travelers*. Cincinnati: Friendship Press, 1995.

Frommer, Arthur. *Arthur Frommer's New World of Travel: A Guide to Alternative Vacations in the Americas and Throughout the World*. New York: Prentice Hall, updated annually.

Gamble, W. P. *Tourism and Development in Africa*. London: Murray, 1989.

Ganga, Gobind. *Ecotourism in Guyana: Implications for Sustainable Development*. Georgetown: University of Guyana, 1994.

Garland, Alex. *The Beach*. New York: Riverhead Books, 1997. Fiction; a story about young Westerners traveling in Southeast Asia and the never-ending search for the last unspoiled idyll.

Gayle, Dennis J., and Jonathan N. Goodrich, eds. *Tourism Marketing and Management in the Caribbean*. London: Routledge, 1993.

Go, Frank M. *Tourism and Economic Development in Asia and Australia*. London: Pinter, 1995.

———, and Ray Pine. *Globalization Strategy in the Hotel Industry*. London: Routledge, 1995.

Gollin, Jim, and Ron Mader. *Honduras: Adventures in Nature*. Santa Fe: John Muir Publications, 1997.

Gonsalves, Paul. *Alternative Tourism: An Operations Manual for Third World Groups*. Bangalore: Equations, 1987.

Graham, Scott. *Handle with Care: A Guide to Responsible Travel in Developing Countries.* Chicago: Noble Press, 1992.

Graphic Arts. *Culture Shock! series.* Portland, OR: Graphic Arts Center Publishing, various years.

Greenpeace. *Impacts of Tourism Development in Pacific Islands.* San Francisco: Greenpeace Pacific Campaign, 1992.

Grotta, Daniel, and Sally Wiener Grotta. *The Green Travel Sourcebook: A Guide for the Physically Active, the Intellectually Curious, or the Socially Aware.* New York: Wiley, 1992.

Hall, C. M. *Tourism and Politics: Policy, Power, and Place.* New York: Wiley, 1994.

———. *Tourism and Public Policy.* London: Routledge, 1995.

———. *Tourism in the Pacific Rim: Development, Impacts, and Markets.* New York: Halstead Press, 1994.

Hall, Michael, and Stephen Page, eds. *Tourism and the Pacific: Issues and Cases.* London: Thomas Business Press, 1996.

Harris, Rob, and Neil Leiper, eds. *Sustainable Tourism: An Australian Perspective.* Oxford: Butterworth-Heinemann, 1995.

Harrison, David, ed. *Tourism and the Less Developed Countries.* New York: Halstead Press, 1992.

Hausler, Nicole, Christina Kamp, Peter Muller-Rockstroh, Wolfgang Scholz, and Barbara E. Schulz, eds. *Retracing the Track of Tourism: Studies on Travels, Tourists and Development.* Saarbrücken, Germany: Verlag für Entwicklungspolitik Breitenbach, 1995.

Hawkins, Donald E., and J. P. Brent Ritchie, eds. *World Travel and Tourism Review: Indicators, Trends and Forecasts.* Wallingford, Oxford: CAB International, 1991.

———, Megan Epler Wood, and Sam Bittman, eds. *The Ecolodge Sourcebook for Planners and Developers.* North Bennington, VT: The Ecotourism Society, 1995.

Hitchcock, Michael, Victor T. King, and Michael J. G. Parnwell, eds. *Tourism in Southeast Asia.* London: Routledge, 1993.

Holing, Dwight. *Earthtrips: A Guide to Nature Travel on a Fragile Planet.* Los Angeles: Conservation International and Living Planet Press, 1991.

———, ed. *World Travel: A Guide to International Ecojourneys.* San Francisco: Nature Company–Time Life Books, 1996.

Hong, Evelyne. *See the Third World While It Lasts: The Social and Environmental Impact of Tourism.* Penang, Malaysia: Consumers' Association of Penang, 1985.

hooks, bell. *Black Looks: Race and Representation.* Boston: South End Press, 1992.

Hubbs, Clay, ed. *Alternative Travel Directory.* Amherst: Transitions Abroad Publishing, annually.

Human Rights Watch. *Burma: Entrenchment or Reform: Human Rights Development and the Need for Continued Pressure.* Washington, DC: Human Rights Watch/Asia Watch, 1995.

Hunter, Colin. *Tourism and the Environment: A Sustainable Relationship?* London: Routledge, 1995.

Inkpen, Gary. *Information Technology for Travel and Tourism*. London: Pitman Publishing, 1994.

Inter-Hemispheric Education Resource Center. *Inside*. Albuquerque, NM: Inter-Hemispheric Resource Center, n.d.

International Resources Group. *Ecotourism: A Viable Alternative for Sustainable Management of Natural Resources in Africa*. Washington, DC: International Resources Group and USAID, 1992.

International Society for Ecology and Culture (ISEC) and the Ladakh Project. *The Future of Progress: Reflections on Environment and Development*. Berkeley: ISEC and the Ladakh Project, 1992.

IUCN: The World Conservation Union. *Paradise on Earth: IUCN/The World Conservation Union (UNESCO) World Heritage Sites*. Washington, DC: IUCN and JIDP Publications, 1995.

Jaimes, Annette, ed. *The State of Native America*. Boston: South End Press, 1992.

Jefferson, Allan, and Leonard Lickorish. *Marketing Tourism: A Practical Guide*. Essex: Longman Group, 1991.

Kincaid, Jamaica. *A Small Place*. New York: PLUME/Penguin Books, 1988.

Kinnaird, Vivian, and Derek Hall, eds. *Tourism: A Gender Analysis*. New York: Wiley, 1994.

Kleymeyer, Charles David, ed. *Cultural Expression and Grassroots Development: Case Studies from Latin America and the Caribbean*. Boulder, CO: Lynne Rienner Publishers, 1994.

Krippendorf, Jost. *The Holiday Makers: Understanding the Impact of Leisure and Travel*. Translated by Vera Andrassy. Oxford: Butterworth-Heinemann, 1994.

Krotz, Larry. *Tourists: How Our Fastest Growing Industry Is Changing the World*. New York: Faber and Faber, 1996.

Lanfant, Marie-Françoise, John B. Allcock, and Edward M. Bruner, eds. *International Tourism: Identity and Change*. Thousand Oak, CA: SAGE Publications, 1995.

Lea, John. *Tourism and Development in the Third World*. London: Routledge, 1988.

Lewand, Alan A., and Lawrence Yu, eds. *Tourism in China*. Boulder, CO: Westview Press, 1995.

Lindberg, Kreg, and Donald Hawkins, eds. *Ecotourism: A Guide for Planners and Managers*. North Bennington, VT: Ecotourism Society, 1993.

Liu, Juanita. *Pacific Islands Ecotourism: A Public Policy and Planning Guide*. Honolulu: Pacific Business Center Program, University of Hawaii, 1991.

MacCannell, Dean. *The Tourist: A New Theory of the Leisure Class*. New York: Shocken Books, 1989.

Madeley, John. *Foreign Exploits: Transnationals and Tourism*. London: Catholic Institute for International Relations, 1995.

Mader, Ron. *Mexico: Adventures in Nature*. Santa Fe: John Muir Publications, 1997.

Mander, Jerry, and Edward Goldsmith, eds. *The Case Against the Global Economy*. San Francisco: Sierra Club Books, 1996.

Marcouiller, David W. *Tourism Planning.* Washington, DC: Council of Planning Librarians, 1995.

Mather, Sue. *Tourism in the Caribbean.* New York: Economist Intelligence Unit, n.d.

McAfee, Kathy. *Storm Signals: Structural Adjustment and Development Alternatives in the Caribbean.* Boston: South End Press, 1991.

McCarthy, John. *Are Sweet Dreams Made of This? Tourism in Bali and Eastern Indonesia.* Northcote, Australia: Indonesian Resources and Information Program (IRIP), 1995.

McDonald, Neil. *The Caribbean: Making Our Own Choices.* Oxford: Oxfam, 1990.

McIntosh, Robert Woodrow, and Charles R. Goeldner. *Tourism: Principles, Practices and Philosophies.* New York: Wiley, 1995.

McIntyre, George. *Sustainable Tourism Development: A Guide for Local Planners.* Madrid: World Tourism Organization, 1993.

Mei-Jung, Yvone Lin, ed. *Asia Consultation on Tourism and Aboriginal Peoples: Community Control, Cultural Dignity and Economic Value.* Taidon, Taiwan: Huadong Community Development Center, 1989.

Mieczkowski, Zbigniew. *Environmental Issues of Tourism and Recreation.* Lanham, MD: University Press of America, 1995.

Momsen, Janet, ed. *Women and Change in the Caribbean.* London: Oxford, 1993.

Montanari, Amanda, and Allen M. Williams, eds. *European Tourism: Regions, Spaces and Restructuring.* New York: Wiley, 1995.

Naisbitt, John. *Global Paradox.* New York: Avon Books, 1994.

Nash, Dennis. *The Anthropology of Tourism.* Oxford: Pergamon Press, 1996.

Nelson, J. G., R. Butler, and G. Wall, eds. *Tourism and Sustainable Development: Monitoring, Planning and Managing.* Ontario: Department of Geography, University of Waterloo, 1993.

Norberg-Hodge, Helena. *Ancient Futures: Learning from Ladakh.* San Francisco: Sierra Club Books, 1991.

O'Grady, Alison, ed. *The Challenge of Tourism: Learning Resources for Study and Action.* Bangkok: Ecumenical Coalition on Third World Tourism, 1990.

O'Grady, Ron. *The Child and the Tourist: The Story Behind the Escalation of Child Prostitution in Asia.* Bangkok: ECPAT, 1992.

———. *Tourism in the Third World: Christian Reflections.* Maryknoll, NY: Orbis Books, 1982.

Partners for Livable Places. *Tourism and Communities: Process, Problems, and Solutions.* Washington, DC: Partners for Livable Places, 1981.

Pattullo, Polly. *Last Resorts: The Cost of Tourism in the Caribbean.* London: Cassell, 1996.

Pearce, Douglas. *Tourism Today: A Geographical Analysis.* New York: Wiley, 1995.

———. *Tourist Development.* New York: Longman Scientific & Technical and Wiley, 1991.

———. *Tourist Organizations.* New York: Longman Scientific & Technical and Wiley, 1992.

Pilarski, Michael. *Friends of the Trees Guide to Hawaii*. Bellingham, WA: Friends of the Trees, 1997.

Pizam, Abraham, and Yoel Mansfeld, eds. *Tourism, Crime, and International Security Issues*. West Sussex: Wiley, 1996.

Poon, Auliana. *Tourism, Technology and Competitive Strategies*. Wallingford, Oxford: CAB International, 1993.

Price, Martin (ed). *Tourism in Fragile Environments*. London: Wesley and Royal Geographic Society, 1996.

Priestly, Gerda K., J. Arwel Edwards, and Harry Coccossis, eds. *Sustainable Development? A European Experience*. Wallingford, Oxford: CAB International, 1996.

Prentice, Richard. *Tourism and Heritage Attractions*. London: Routledge, 1993.

Rames, K. T. *Structural Adjustment, World Trade and Third World Tourism: An Introduction to the Issues*. Bangkok: ECTWT, 1995.

Reed, Ralph Thomas. *American Express: Its Origin and Growth*. New York: Newcomen Society in North America, 1952.

Richter, Linda K. *The Politics of Tourism in Asia*. Honolulu: University of Hawaii Press, 1989.

Rohter, Ira. *Envisioning a Green Hawaii: Two Futures*. Honolulu: Hawaii Green Party, 1992.

Rossel, Pierre, ed. *Tourism: Manufacturing the Exotic*. Copenhagen: International Work Group for Indigenous Affairs, 1988.

Shaw, Gareth, and Allan Williams, eds. *The Rise and Fall of British Coastal Resorts: Cultural and Economic Perspectives*. London: Pinter, 1996.

Sheldon, Pauline. *Tourism Information Systems*. Wallingford, Oxford: CAB International, 1997.

Sinclair, M. Thea, and M. J. Stabler, eds. *The Tourism Industry: An International Analysis*. Wallingford, Oxford: CAB International, 1991.

Singh, Tej Vir, H. Leon Theuns, and Frank M. Go. *Towards Appropriate Tourism: The Case of Developing Countries*. New York: Peter Lang, 1989.

Smith, Stephen L. J. *Tourism Analysis: A Handbook*. Essex: Longman Scientific & Technical, 1995.

Smith, Valene L., ed. *Hosts and Guests: The Anthropology of Tourism*. Philadelphia: University of Pennsylvania Press, 1989.

————, and William R. Eadington, eds. *Tourism Alternatives: Potentials and Problems in the Development of Tourism*. Philadelphia: University of Pennsylvania Press, 1992.

South Pacific Peoples' Foundation. *Tourism: The Pacific Way*. Victoria, BC, Canada: South Pacific Peoples' Foundation, 1994.

Sterling, Claire. *Thieves' World: The Threat of the New Global Network of Organized Crime*. New York: Simon & Schuster, 1994.

Suresh, K. T., ed. *Tourism Issues in Public Domain*. Bangalore: Equations, 1994.

Taylor, Frank Fonda. *To Hell with Paradise: A History of the Jamaican Tourist Industry*. Pittsburgh: University of Pittsburgh Press, 1993.

Trask, Haunani Kay. *From a Native Daughter*. Monroe, ME: Common Courage Press, 1990.

Travel Industry Association of America. *Discover America: Tourism and the Environment: A Guide to Challenges and Opportunities for the Travel Industry Businesses*. Washington, DC: Travel Industry Association of America, 1992.

Truong, Thanh-Dam. *Sex, Money and Morality: Prostitution and Tourism in Southeast Asia*. London: Zed Books, 1990.

Tuting, Ludmilla, and Kunda Dixint, eds. *Bikas-Binas Development: The Change in Life and Environment in the Himalayas*. Varanasi: Jauhari Printers, 1991.

United Nations Environment Programme (UNEP). *Ecotourism in the Wider Caribbean Region: An Assessment*. New York: UNEP, Caribbean Environment Programme, 1994.

————. *Environmental Codes of Conduct for Tourism*. Paris: UNEP, 1991.

University of Colorado and U.S. Travel Data Center. *Tourism's Top Twenty: Fast Facts on Travel and Tourism*. Washington, DC: University of Colorado and U.S. Travel Data Center, 1992.

University of Dublin. *Tourism on the Farm: Proceedings of Two Conferences on Farm Tourism in Ireland*. Enniskillen Fermanagh: University of Dublin, Environmental Institute, 1992.

University of Hawaii. *Ecological Tourism and Small Business in the Pacific*. Honolulu: Pacific Business Center, University of Hawaii, 1991.

————. *The Ecotourism Planning Kit: A Business Planning Guide for Ecotourism Operators in the Pacific Islands*. Honolulu: University of Hawaii, 1994.

University of Waterloo. *Ecotourism: An Annotated Bibliography, Department of Recreation and Leisure Studies*. Waterloo, Ontario: University of Waterloo, 1992.

UnTourist Publications. *UnTourist Guides*. Grand Mackerel Beach, New South Wales, Australia: UnTourist Publications, various years.

Urry, John. *The Tourist Gaze: Leisure and Travel in Contemporary Societies*. Newbury Park, CA: Sage Publications, 1990.

U.S. Forest Service. *Tourism on Federal Lands: A Resource Book*. Washington, DC: U.S. Forest Service, 1992.

U.S. Travel and Trade Administration (USTTA). *World Tourism at the Millennium: An Agenda for Industry, Government and Education*. Washington, DC: USTA, 1993.

U.S. Travel Data Center. *Travel Market Close-Up*. Washington, DC: U.S. Travel Data Center, 1988–1990.

————. *Travel Market Report: National Travel Survey Tabulations and Analysis*. Washington, DC: U.S. Travel Data Center, annually.

————. *Travel Printout*. Washington, DC: U.S. Travel Data Center, annually.

Van den Berghe, Pierre L. *Quest for the Other: Ethnic Tourism in San Cristobal, Mexico*. Seattle: University of Washington Press, 1994.

Van Harsell, Jan. *Tourism: An Exploration*. Englewood Cliffs, NJ: National Publishers of the Black Hills and Prentice-Hall, 1982.

Vellas, François, and Lionel Bechard. *International Tourism: An Economic*

Perspective. New York: St. Martin's Press, 1995.

Vintage Departures. A series of nonfiction travel accounts that illustrate many aspects of travel and tourism. Published by Vintage Books, a division of Random House. Sample titles: Pico Iyer, *Video Night in Kathmandu*; Redmond O'Hanlon, *Into the Heart of Borneo*; Vikram Seth, *From Heaven Lake*.

Volunteers for Peace. *International Work Camp Directory*. Belmont, VT: Volunteers for Peace, 1997.

Weiler, Betty, and Colin Michael Hall, eds. *Special Interest Tourism*. London: Bellhaven Press, 1992.

Wheatcroft, Stephen. *Aviation and Tourism Policies: Balancing the Benefits*. London: Routledge, 1994.

Whelan, Tensie, ed. *Nature Tourism: Managing for the Environment*. Washington, DC: Island Press, 1991.

White, Kenneth J. *Tourism and the Antarctic Economy*. Vancouver: University of British Columbia, 1993.

Wilson, Kemmons. *The Holiday Inn Story*. New York: Newcomen Society in North America, 1968.

World Bank and UNESCO. *Tourism: Passport to Development? Perspectives on the Social and Cultural Impacts of Tourism in Developing Countries*. London: Oxford University Press, 1979.

World Tourism Organization. *Budgets and Marketing Plans of National Tourism Administrations*. Madrid: World Tourism Organization, 1995.

———. *Collection of Domestic Tourism Statistics*. Madrid: World Tourism Organization, 1995.

———. *Compendium of Tourism Statistics*. Madrid: World Tourism Organization, annually.

———. *Guidelines: Development of National Parks and Protected Areas for Tourism*. Madrid: World Tourism Organization and the United Nations Environment Programme, 1992.

———. *Tourism Market Trends: East Asia and the Pacific*. Madrid: World Tourism Organization, Commission for East Asia and the Pacific, 1995.

———. *Tourism Market Trends: Middle East, 1980–1993*. Madrid: World Tourism Organization, Commission for the Middle East, 1994.

———. *Tourism Safety and Security: Practical Measures for Destinations*. Madrid: World Tourism Organization, 1996.

World Travel and Tourism Council. *Travel and Tourism: Progress and Priorities 1995*. Madrid: World Travel and Tourism Council, 1995.

Young, Elspeth. *Third World in the First: Development and Indigenous Peoples*. London: Routledge, 1995.

Ziffer, Karen A. *Ecotourism: The Uneasy Alliance*. Washington, DC: Conservation International and Ernst & Young, 1989.

Zurich, David. *Hawaii Naturally: An Environmentally Oriented Guide to the Wonders and Pleasures of the Islands*. Berkeley: Wilderness Press, 1990.

guides for students

Funding for U.S. Study, and Financial Resources for International Study: A Guide for U.S. Students and Professionals. IIE Books, PO Box 371, Annapolis Junction, MD 20701-0371.

A Guide to Israel Programs. World Zionist Organization, 110 E. Street, 3rd Floor, New York, NY 10022; (800) 274-7723.

Multi-Cultural Tourism Development Workbook. Western Entrepreneurial Network, Colorado Center for Community Development, University of Colorado at Denver, PO Box 173364, Campus Box 128, Denver, CO 80217-3364. Indicate specialized area: African American, Asian American, Hispanic American, Native American; each comes with video case study.

Opportunities in Africa. Interbook, 130 Cedar Street, New York, NY 10006.

Routledge Introductions to Development. John Bale and Dave Drakakis-Smith, eds. Routledge, 11 New Fetter Lane, London 4P 433, UK, or Routledge, Chapman and Hall, Inc. 29 W. 35th Street, New York, NY 10001. Series of introductory books for students includes *Tourism and Development in the Third World* by John Lea.

Writing Your Dissertation on Sustainable Tourism. Tourism Concern, Stapleton House, 277-281 Holloway Road, London N7 8HN, UK; 44-171-753-3330, fax 44-171-753-3331, tourconcern@gn.apc.org.

web sites

responsible tourism sites

Environment and Latin American Network
■ http://csf.Colorado.EDU/ mail/elan/

Millennium Institute
■ http://www.igc.upc.org/millennium

One World Partnership
■ http://www.oneworld.org/news/world/tourism.html

Tourism Concern
■ http://www.oneworld.org/tourconcern

World Views
■ gopher://gopher.igc.apc.org:70/oo/orgs/worldviews/ tourism.igc or http://www.igc.org.worldviews

ecotourism sites

Belize Online: Ecotourism Ethics
■ http://www.belize.com/eco.html

Canadian National Aboriginal Tourism
■ http://www.vli.ca/clients/abc/cnata/directory.htm

Center for Nature & Heritage Tourism
- http://www.cybercorp.net/~ecotourism

Civilized Explorer
- http://www.crl.com/~philip/advntr.html/

Earthwyz Journeys
- http://www.teleport.com/~earthwyz/

EcoNET
- http://www.wttc.org/

Eco-Orbit
- http://public-www.pi.se/%7Eorbit/eco.html

Eco-Source
- http://www.podi.com/ecosource/

Ecotourism
- http://www2.planeta.com/mader/ecotravel/etour.html.

Ecotourism in the Pacific Asia Region
- http://www.for.nau.edu/~alew/ecotsvy.html

Ecotourism Operator Guide
- http://www.txinfinet.com/mader/planeta/0597/0597operators.html

Ecotourism Resource Site
- http://www.vuw.ac.nz/~agsmith/847/resguide/craven/eco.htm

Eco-Travel
- http://www.teleport com/

Ecoventure
- http://134.121.164.23/ecoventure.htm

Eco Voyager
- http://www.ecovoyager.com/

GORP
- http//www.gorp.com

Green Arrow's Conservation Connection
- http://www.greenarrow.com/nature/connect.htm

Green Arrow Guide to Central America Ecotourism
- http://www.greenarrow.com/ecohome.htm

Green.Travel
- http://www.igc.org/igc/peacenet/index.html

Green Travel
- http://www.green-travel.com and http://www.infotec-travel.com

Green Travel Archives/mailing list
- gopher://ecosys.drdr.virginia.edu

Hawaii Ecotourism Association
- http://www.planet-hawaii.com/hea/

Honduras Unplugged
- http://www2.planeta.com/mader/planeta/0597/0597.html

International SeaCanoe
- http://seacanoe.com/

Kenya-Nepal Ecotourism
- http://www.nrdc.org/amicus96/etnep3.html

Legacy International-Sustainable Tourism
- http://www.infi.net/~legacy/

Maui Eco Directory Map and Guide
- http://www.planet-hawaii.com/ecomap/

National Park Service
- http://www.nps.gov/

El Planeta: Ecotravels in Latin America
- http://www.planeta.com/

One World Partnership
- www.oneworld.org/news/world/tourism.html

Outahere Travel Guide
- http://www.outahere.com/

Planeta Platica
- http://www2.planeta.com/mader/planeta/planeta_current.html

Samoan Ecotourism Network
- http://www.pi.se/~orbit/samoa/welcome.html

Study Group on Sustainable Tourism
- http://www.for.nau.edu/geography/igust

Thoho-ku (Mexico) Ecological Projects
- http://www.expo-yucatan.com/index.htm

Vapour Trails Online Travel
- http://www.vaportrails.com/

ecotourism programs

Alaska Wilderness Recreation and Tourism Association
- http://www.alaska.net:80/~awrta/

Audubon Expedition Institute and Lesley College
- http://www.audubon.org/audubon/aei.html

Conservation International
- http://www.conservation.org/

Earthwatch
- http://gaia.earthwatch.org/WWW/Tskills.html

GreenTracks
- http://www.gorp.com/greentracks/ or
  http://www.herp.com/grtrack/grntrack.html

Hoso-Kallbygden, Swedish EcoVillage
- http://www.sbbs.se/hp/hkab

International Expeditions
- http://www.icsys.com/intexp/

Journeys International
- http://www.gorp.com/journeys.htm

Kodukant Ecotourism Initiative, Estonia
- http://www.ee/kodukant/ecotourism

Kuda Laut/Scuba Ecotourism and Marine Biology
- http://www.wp.com/kudalaut/

Specialty Travel Index
- http://www.spectrav.com/

ecotourism research and papers

Can Ecotourism Save Rainforests?
- http://www.ran.org/ran/info_center/ecotourism.html

Challenge Ecotourism
- http://www.txinfinet.com/mader/planeta/0295/0295shores.html

Cultural Resources and Sustainable Tourism
- http://www.al.net/endotourism.html

Ecotourism
- http://www.africa.com/satour/page15c.htm

Ecotourism Industry Statistics
- http://www.podi.com/ecosource/industry.htm

Eco-tourism or Eco-terrorism?
- http://www.nornet.on.ca/%7Ejharnick/tourism.html

Ecotourism: Paradise Gained or Lost?
- http://www.oneworld.org/panos/panos_eco2.html

Ecotourism Research in Ecuador
- http://www.geog.umn.edu/~schaller/

Elsevier Science Catalogue (Tourism Resources)
- http://www.elsevier.nl/

Independent Research Organizations
- http://www.bcu.ubc.ca/~megill/res_orgs_hp.html

Indigenous Ecotourism/UREP
- http://www.mip.berkeley.edu/urep/susdev.html

Indigenous Ecotourism and Sustainable Development
- http://www.geog.umn.edu/~schaller/

International Center for Ecotourism Research
- http://www.gu.edu.au/gwis/icer/icer_home.html

Samoan Ecotourism Network
- http://www.odyssey.com.au/uspecies/orbit/eco.html

Two Way Track–Australia
- http://www.kaos.erin.gov.au/life/general_info/biodivser_5/twoch6.html

general travel information

Around the World
- http://www.solutions.net/rec-travel/rtw/html/faq.html

Business Travel–International Student Travel Confederation
- http://www.istc.org/

EcoVillage
- http://www.sbbs.se/hp/hkab/

Explorer's Guide/Virtual Village
- http://www.desocom.com/

GORP (Great Outdoor Recreation Pages)
- http://www.gorp.com/

InfoHub
- http://www.infohub.com/

Kenn Nesbitt's Travel
- http://www.thegroup.net/kenn.htm

National Park Travel Guide
- http://www.pe.net/~glfoote/

Travel and Tourism
- http://222.akebono.stanford.edu/yahoo/government.countries

Travel Source
- http://www.travelsource.com/

Trip Finder
- http://www.travelon.com/

Virtual North: Adventures in Canada
- http://www.virtualnorth.com/vn.html

Virtual Tourist World Map
- http://wings.buffalo.edu/world/

World Wide Wilderness Directory
- http://www.wbm.ca/wilderness/

general sources of environmental information

Amazing Environmental Organization Web
- http://www.webdirectory.com/

EcoNet
- http://www.igc.apc.org/econet/

Environmental Organizations On-Line
- http://envirolink.org/orgs/index.html

environmental/developmental organizations on the web

Association for the Conservation of Nature
- http://www.fcn.org/

Bicycle Africa
- http://www.halcyon.com/fkroger/bike/bikeafr.htm

Center for Alternative Technology
- http://www.oneworld.org/jobs/index.html

Corporate Watch
- http://www.corpwatch.org or http://www.corpwatch.org/corner/alert/

Earth Island Institute–Sea Turtle Project
- http://www.earthisland.org/ei/strpindx.html

Earth Pledge Foundation
- http://www.earthpledge.org/

Friends of the Earth
- http://www.foe.co.uk/

Global Response
- http://www.globalresponse.org/

International Bicycle Fund
- http://www.halcyon.comfkroger/bike/homepage.html

International Bike Route Directory
- http://www.BikeRoute.com/

International Development Research Center
- http://www.idrc.ca/index.html

International Institute for Sustainable Development
- http://iisd1.iisd.ca/

International Peace Through Tourism
- http://www.nolimits.com/nolimits/iipt.html

National Bicycle Greenway
- http://www.BikeRoute.com/

National Parks and Conservation Association
- http://www.npca.com/pub/npca/wwwhome.html

Rainforest Action Network
- http://www.ran.org/ran/index.html

Sierra Club
- http://www.sierraclub.org/

Sierra Club Policy on Ecotourism
- http://www.sierraclub.org/policy/722.html

Sustainable Island Information Network
- http://www.upei.ca/~siin/tourism.htm

Transnational Resource and Action Center (TRAC)
- http://www.corpwatch.org/

Wilderness Society
- http://town.hall.org/environment/wild_soc/wilders. html

World Resources Institute
- http://www.ciesin.org/IC/wri/wrihome.html

World Wildlife Fund
- http://www.envirolink.org/orgs/wqed/wwf/wwf_home.html

index

about the author

DEBORAH MCLAREN is the Director of the Rethinking Tourism Project, a non-profit education and networking project that supports Indigenous self-development, as well as a columnist who writes about environmentally and socially responsible tourism for *Transitions Abroad*. Ms. McLaren earned her master's degree in social ecology from Goddard College. She has lived and worked throughout Asia and the Americas and resides in Washington, D.C.

Currently she is organizing educational exchanges between Indigenous Peoples to work together on tourism issues, designing educational programs that integrate Indigenous science and wisdom, and recruiting Indigenous Peoples and others to work on international tourism policy and research. She believes critical new areas of research include monitoring the multilateral financial institutions' tourism investments and development and new ideas for cooperative land management partnerships between Native groups and governments.